SHAKING THE FOUNDATION

Charles Darwin and the Theory of EVOLUTION

SYLVIA A. JOHNSON

TFCB

TWENTY-FIRST CENTURY BOOKS / MINNEAPOLIS

Twenty-First Century Books
A division of Lerner Publishing Group, Inc.
241 First Avenue North
Minneapolis, MN 55401 U.S.A.

Website address: www.lernerbooks.com

Library of Congress Cataloging-in-Publication Data

Johnson, Sylvia A.
Shaking the foundation : Charles Darwin and the theory of evolution / by Sylvia A. Johnson.
p.   cm.
Includes bibliographical references and index.
ISBN 978–0–7613–5486–4 (lib. bdg. : alk. paper)
1. Evolution (Biology)—Juvenile literature.
2. Darwin, Charles, 1809–1882—Juvenile literature.
I. Title.
QH367.1.J64 2013
576.8'2—dc23   2012018075

Manufactured in the United States of America
1 – BP – 12/31/12

CONTENTS

IN THE BEGINNING, GOD CREATED THE HEAVENS AND THE EARTH.... AND GOD SAID, "LET THE WATERS BRING FORTH ABUNDANTLY THE MOVING CREATURE THAT HATH LIFE.... AND GOD CREATED GREAT WHALES... AND EVERY WINGED FOWL AFTER HIS KIND.... AND GOD MADE THE BEAST OF THE EARTH AFTER HIS KIND, AND CATTLE AFTER THEIR KIND.

—Gen. 1:20, 21, 25 (King James Version)

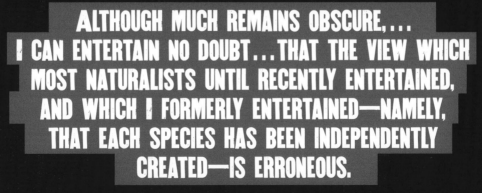

2

4

Charles Darwin made these illustrations of four different types of finches while exploring the Galápagos Islands in the 1830s. Each bird was uniquely adapted for the environment of the island on which it lived.

ALTHOUGH MUCH REMAINS OBSCURE,...
I CAN ENTERTAIN NO DOUBT...THAT THE VIEW WHICH
MOST NATURALISTS UNTIL RECENTLY ENTERTAINED,
AND WHICH I FORMERLY ENTERTAINED—NAMELY,
THAT EACH SPECIES HAS BEEN INDEPENDENTLY
CREATED—IS ERRONEOUS.

—**Charles Darwin,** *On the Origin of Species,* **1859**

The questions could not have been more basic. Where did all the varied forms of life on Earth come from: fish in the seas, birds in the air, plants and animals on land, and humans themselves?

Did an all-powerful God create each species, or kind, individually, as described in the Book of Genesis?

Charles Darwin *(above)* **published the groundbreaking book** *On the Origin of Species* **in 1859. The book proposed new ideas about the origins of life at a time of enormous social change and scientific advancement.**

Or was the view based on this account wrong, as Charles Darwin claimed in his famous book *On the Origin of Species?* Could there be some other explanations for the origin of the "endless forms most beautiful and most wonderful" that filled the world?

An age of revolution

During the early 1800s, many people in Great Britain and Europe had begun to reexamine the questions surrounding the origin of life. The events of previous decades had shaken the foundations of Western society. Beliefs held in the past no longer seemed so certain.

In 1776 the British colonies in North America had rebelled against the crown and declared their independence. Inspired by the American Revolution (1775–1783), French citizens revolted against their own government in 1789. During the bloody revolution that followed, a king and a queen were executed. In 1798 the French general Napoleon Bonaparte began his campaign of conquest against the armies of Europe and Great Britain. The Napoleonic Wars began in 1803 and lasted twelve long years until Bonaparte was defeated in 1815.

In the early 1800s, some in Great Britain had feared that revolution might break out in their country. This did not happen. Nevertheless, there were riots and demands for reform in government during this period that made the ruling class uneasy.

The Industrial Revolution began in Great Britain in the mid-1700s. By the mid-1800s, machine-based manufacturing had spread to western Europe, North America, and other parts of the world. This image shows workers at a textile mill, where machines are making cotton thread.

In the 1650s, James Ussher, a bishop of the Anglican Church in Ireland, proclaimed that God had created the world in the year 4004 B.C. He reached this conclusion by adding up the life spans of Methuselah and other descendants of Adam mentioned in the Book of Genesis. Ussher's date was widely accepted by church leaders and many scientists. It was often included in editions of the King James Bible.

Some of the greatest changes affecting Great Britain came in the economy. The Industrial Revolution was beginning to transform the country from a land of farms and villages to a nation of factories and industrial towns. Powered by coal-fired steam engines, new machines were producing everything from cotton cloth to iron parts for the newly built railroads. Thousands of people left their farms and villages to work in factories in the nation's fast-growing industrial cities.

Profits from the production of goods created a new and prosperous middle class. Yet industrialization did not benefit everyone. Workers did not earn enough to afford the products they were making. They often lived in dirty, crowded housing where disease was common. As a result of the Industrial Revolution, British society became deeply divided.

NEW QUESTIONS, NEW IDEAS

During this period of change, religion was also questioned. Scientists had begun to construct a picture of the world that was very different from the one presented in the Christian Bible. During the 1700s, many Christians believed that the creation of Earth had happened within the last ten thousand years. By the early 1800s, however, most educated people knew that this could not be true. Researchers in France and in Great Britain had begun to study the many layers of rock that make up the surface of Earth. They realized that it would have taken much longer than a few thousand years for these layers to have been deposited.

The discovery of the remains of unfamiliar animals within the different layers led to further questions. In 1796 French naturalist Georges Cuvier examined fossils of mammoths found in Europe. He declared that they were the remains of animals that had become extinct thousands of years ago. He also studied the fossilized skeletons of other extinct animals, including a giant sloth and a mastodon. Later, fossils of dinosaurs would be discovered.

According to Christian tradition, God made all plants and animals during the six days described in the Book of Genesis. His creation was complete and perfect and could never change. But the fossil record indicated that some living things had become extinct. New forms of life had also appeared. How could this be possible?

Georges Cuvier thought that periodic floods were responsible for killing off living creatures over time. A few animals and plants survived to repopulate the world. Some Christian thinkers who accepted this catastrophic view of Earth's history suggested that God created life anew after each disaster. The account in Genesis, they said, described just one of these creations. This answer did not satisfy traditional Christians, who were opposed to Cuvier's ideas.

THEORIES OF TRANSMUTATION

Jean-Baptiste Lamarck, a French naturalist and contemporary of Cuvier, had his own theory about the origins of life. He did not believe in a world shaped by catastrophes. According to Lamarck's theory, living things did not become extinct. Instead, they gradually changed in response to changes in the environment. Eventually they developed into new and different creatures. Lamarck called this process transmutation.

Lamarck described his theory in a book published in 1809.

French naturalist Georges Cuvier (*below*) was fascinated with the anatomy of animals. He is known for studies comparing living animals with fossils of their ancestors and for establishing extinction as a scientific reality.

This sketch of the skeleton of an African sacred ibis (*left*) is from a paper Cuvier published in 1804.

In his 1809 book *Zoological Philosophy*, Jean-Baptiste Lamarck proposed his idea of evolution, in which species evolve over time in response to their environments. This is the title page of an 1850 French edition of the book.

His ideas were not widely accepted by European scientists, who generally supported Cuvier's views. A few years earlier, transmutation had been introduced in Great Britain by Erasmus Darwin, Charles Darwin's grandfather. Darwin, who was a poet as well as a physician and a botanist, described his ideas about transmutation in a book titled *Zoonomia*.

When Erasmus Darwin's grandson Charles was born in 1809, transmutation was an idea familiar to many. Educated people were already discussing the way in which living things change and develop over time. It would not be long before a new and powerful voice would join the discussion.

Chapter One

ENTER CHARLES DARWIN

Charles Robert Darwin was born on February 12, 1809, in Shrewsbury, England. He was the fifth child and second son of Susannah Darwin and Robert Darwin. Robert was a physician like his father, Erasmus. Susannah had been born into the wealthy Wedgwood family. Josiah Wedgwood I, Susannah's father, had made his fortune in the manufacturing of pottery. Like the Darwins, the Wedgwoods were educated people who were liberals in politics and religion.

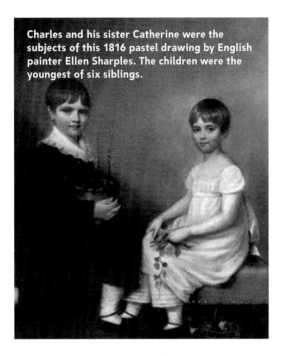

Charles and his sister Catherine were the subjects of this 1816 pastel drawing by English painter Ellen Sharples. The children were the youngest of six siblings.

Susannah Darwin died when Charles was only nine. In his autobiography, he claimed that he remembered "hardly anything about her except her death-bed." Charles was raised by his older sisters and his father, who had a powerful influence on his life. A very successful doctor, Robert Darwin was also "a cautious and good man of business," according to his son. Charles respected his distinguished father but also felt intimidated by him.

MEDICINE OR THE CHURCH?

Robert Darwin wanted both Charles and his older brother, Erasmus, to become physicians. After a not very impressive career at private grammar schools, in 1825 Charles set off for the medical school at Edinburgh University in Scotland. He was only sixteen years old, but it was not unusual in this period for boys to go to a university at an early age.

Charles Darwin's medical training in Edinburgh was not a success. He found the lectures boring and the surgical

Charles Darwin began his distinguished career as a scientist by studying medicine. He later attended Cambridge University, where he took courses in natural history and theology. This photograph of Darwin was taken in 1854, five years before the publication of *On the Origin of Species*.

demonstrations disturbing. He did enjoy lectures on chemistry, geology, and zoology, and he joined a society of students interested in science. Charles also became friends with Robert Grant, a lecturer in the medical school. Grant was an enthusiastic supporter of Lamarck's views on transmutation.

After two years, Charles Darwin left Edinburgh. He was convinced that he was not cut out to be a physician. His father agreed and proposed that he try another career—clergyman in the Church of England, or Anglican Church. Many educated young men in the early 1800s found professions in the church. They became vicars (pastors) in country parishes where their religious duties were light. Country vicars had time to hunt, study natural history, and write.

Charles Darwin was at first uncertain about being a clergyman. He did not think he could accept all the beliefs of the Church of England. Eventually, however, Darwin decided that he did not "in the least doubt the strict and literal truth of every word in the Bible." He was ready to take up this new career.

FAMILY HISTORY

In the 1870s, Charles Darwin wrote a short account of his life for his children. His son Francis included parts of this "autobiography" in *Life and Letters of Charles Darwin*, published after Darwin's death. At the urging of family members, Francis omitted material considered too revealing, particularly his father's religious views. The complete and uncensored autobiography did not appear in print until 1958.

Like most young men in training to be Anglican clergymen, Charles Darwin first had to earn an undergraduate degree. In 1828 he went to Cambridge University in England. There, he studied theology, mathematics, and classics. He also found time to pursue his interest in natural history. Darwin attended lectures by John Henslow, a professor of botany. He learned about geology from Adam Sedgwick, another young Cambridge professor.

In his two years at Cambridge, Darwin did not neglect his social life.

"I . . . saw two very bad operations, one on a child, but I rushed away before they were completed. Nor did I ever attend again, for hardly any inducement would have been strong enough to make me do so; this being long before the blessed days of chloroform. The two cases haunted me for many a long year."

—Charles Darwin, mid-1870s

Francis Darwin (above), son of Charles Darwin, published the book Life and Letters of Charles Darwin after his father's death.

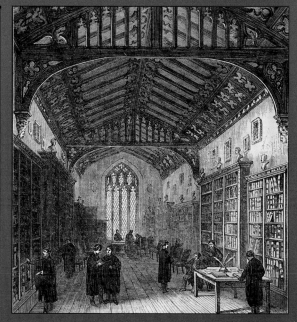

Darwin's memories of his early education at Shrewsbury School (above) in Shrewsbury, England, were not pleasant. The school was very strict and did not encourage his interest in the sciences. He later said that thinking about the smell of the school dormitory made him feel nauseous.

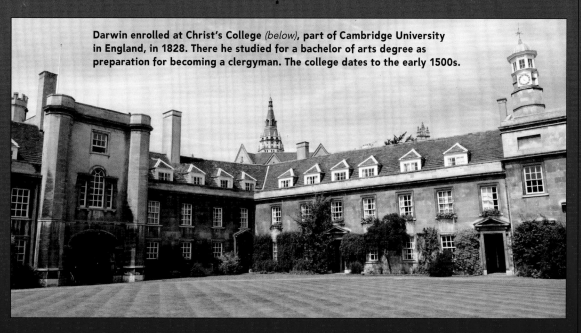

Darwin enrolled at Christ's College (below), part of Cambridge University in England, in 1828. There he studied for a bachelor of arts degree as preparation for becoming a clergyman. The college dates to the early 1500s.

He became part of a "sporting set" of students dedicated to shooting and hunting. One of his companions was his second cousin William Darwin Fox, who was also training to become a clergyman. Fox introduced Darwin to a new and absorbing pastime: collecting beetles. Charles spent hours exploring the countryside around Cambridge, looking for new species to add to his collection.

Darwin earned his bachelor of arts degree in 1831. He would return to Cambridge in the autumn to begin his theological studies. Meanwhile, a long summer stretched ahead of him. In August he accompanied geology professor Adam Sedgwick on a field trip to study ancient rocks in Wales. When Darwin returned to his home in Shrewsbury, he found a letter waiting for him that would change his life.

THE *BEAGLE* ADVENTURE

The letter was from John Henslow, Darwin's botany teacher. Henslow had heard about an opportunity for research and exploration that seemed perfect for his young friend. A British surveying ship, the HMS *Beagle*, was preparing to set off on a voyage around the world. Its captain, Robert FitzRoy, was looking for a naturalist to join the crew. Captain FitzRoy insisted that the naturalist had to be an educated "gentleman" since he would be dining with the captain and spending leisure time with him.

The twenty-three-year-old Darwin was eager to take advantage of this unusual opportunity, but his father disapproved. Nevertheless, he told Charles, "If you can find any man of common sense who advises you to go, I will give my consent." Charles appealed to his uncle Jos (Josiah Wedgwood II). Wedgwood convinced Robert Darwin to support his son's plans.

On December 27, 1831, the HMS *Beagle* departed from the port of Plymouth and headed out into the Atlantic Ocean. Its destination was South America. There its crew would chart the waters off the southern coast of the continent for the British navy. The *Beagle* was a small sailing ship, 90 feet (27 meters) long and 24 feet (7.3 m) at its widest spot. The cabin that Darwin shared with

Darwin was an unpaid naturalist aboard the HMS *Beagle* (above) on its five-year voyage (1831–1836) around the globe. During the expedition, Darwin collected a variety of scientific information that he used to develop his theory of evolution.

Botany professor John Henslow *(above)* was a key mentor in Darwin's life. It was he who suggested Darwin join the crew of the HMS *Beagle* and make the trip that would forever change Darwin's life and career.

two other shipmates was tiny.

During the *Beagle*'s five-year voyage, Charles Darwin experienced violent tropical storms, freezing temperatures, an earthquake, shipwrecks, and even a revolution. While the ship was at sea, he suffered acutely from seasickness. Despite these hardships, Darwin later said that the *Beagle* voyage was "the most important event in my life and . . . determined my whole career. . . . [It was] the first real training or education of my mind."

Robert FitzRoy (1805–1865) was the captain of the *Beagle*. He was an English naval officer and a meteorologist at the forefront of developing the science of forecasting the weather.

LEARNING FROM NATURE

As the *Beagle* began its survey work, Darwin took every opportunity to go ashore. On land he could escape from seasickness and explore. He often spent weeks at a time traveling on horseback and catching up with the *Beagle* as it made its slow way down the coast. During these trips, he collected thousands of specimens of plants, insects, birds, and mammals. The specimens were preserved and stored on board the *Beagle* until they could be sent back to John Henslow in England. Darwin also kept a detailed record of all his finds in his journals. He was particularly interested in the differences as well as similarities that could be observed among species from the same region.

On his expeditions, Darwin also paid close attention to the land itself. Since his Cambridge days, he had been fascinated by geology. In South America, he had a whole new world of rocks and mountains to explore. One of the books Darwin had with him was a volume on geology written by Charles Lyell. Lyell's *Principles of Geology* claimed that the ancient Earth had not been shaped by violent floods and other catastrophic events. Instead, Earth had changed slowly and gradually. The forces that had brought about the changes were the same ones operating in the present: weather, erosion, earthquakes, and volcanoes.

Darwin was impressed by Lyell's theory of gradual change, known as uniformitarianism. In South America, he found evidence supporting Lyell's ideas in the rock layers of the Andes Mountains. When Darwin experienced an earthquake near the city of Concepción on the west coast of South America, he understood how this natural force could change the shape of the land. "A bad earthquake at once destroys our oldest associations," he wrote in his journal. "The earth, the very emblem of solidity, has moved beneath our feet like a thin crust over a fluid."

CHARLES LYELL

Sir Charles Lyell (1797–1875) was an influential British scientist and a good friend to Charles Darwin. Lyell began his career as a lawyer but soon turned to the study of geology. His ideas were influenced by the work of James Hutton (1726–1797), a Scottish geologist who had first developed the theory of uniformitarianism. Like Hutton, Lyell believed that "the present is the key to the past."

ENCHANTED ISLANDS

By 1835 the surveying work of the *Beagle* crew was finished.

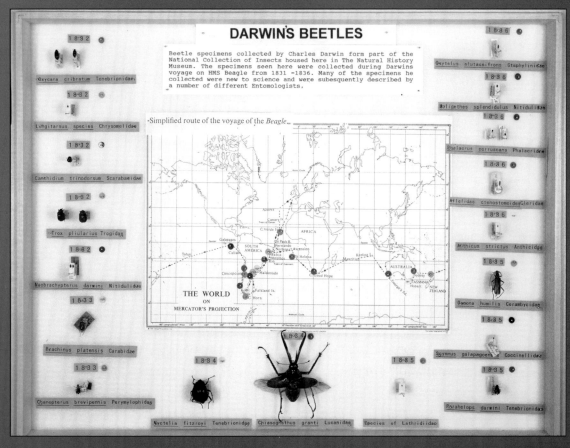

DARWIN'S BEETLES

Beetle specimens collected by Charles Darwin form part of the National Collection of Insects housed here in The Natural History Museum. The specimens seen here were collected during Darwins voyage on HMS Beagle from 1831 -1836. Many of the specimens he collected were new to science and were subsequently described by a number of different Entomologists.

Simplified route of the voyage of the *Beagle*

THE WORLD ON MERCATOR'S PROJECTION

Oxycara cribratum Tenebrionidae.

Longitarsus species Chrysomelidae

Canthidium trinodorsum Scarabaeidae

Trox plularius Trogidae

Neobrachypterus darwini Nitidulidae

Brachinus platensis Carabidae

Chanopterus brevipennis Perymylophidae

Oxytelus alutaceifrons Staphylinidae

Meligethes splendidulus Nitidulidae

Phalacrus corruscans Phalacridae

Allelidea ctenostomoides Cleridae

Anthicus strictus Anthicidae

Oemona humilis Cerambycidae

Scymnus galapagoem Coccinellidae

Parahelops darwini Tenebrionidae

Nyctelia fitzroyi Tenebrionidae   Chiasognathus granti Lucanidae   Species of Lathridiidae

---

On the *Beagle* expedition, Darwin collected a wide range of specimens, including these beetles. The map shows the route the ship took on its famous journey.

In December 1832, the *Beagle* visited Tierra del Fuego, at the southern tip of South America. Darwin was fascinated by the peoples who lived in this cold and rocky land. This illustration of those peoples was drawn by *Beagle* captain Robert FitzRoy and was published as part of a larger book in 1838.

In September 1835, before departing for the long journey home, the ship made a stop in the Galápagos Islands. This archipelago (group of islands) is 600 miles (965 kilometers) off the coast of Peru. Darwin had heard that the fourteen islands were inhabited by many strange forms of wildlife. He was eager to visit them.

As Darwin and the *Beagle* crew explored the rugged terrain of the islands, they encountered giant tortoises. The animals were so large it took six or eight men to lift them. They also saw thousands of iguanas, some living only on land and others swimming in the sea. The islands were home to many kinds of birds, including finches and mockingbirds. They were so tame that they could often be captured by hand. Darwin collected hundreds of bird specimens and prepared the skins to be sent back to England.

Darwin was fascinated and puzzled by what he saw in the Galápagos Islands. In his journal, he summarized his views:

> *The natural history of these islands is eminently curious.... Most of the organic productions are aboriginal [native] creations, found nowhere else; there is even a difference between the inhabitants of the different islands; yet all show a marked relationship with those of America, though separated from that continent by an open ocean.... The archipelago is a little world within itself.*

After leaving the Galápagos Islands in October 1835, the *Beagle* made stops in Tahiti, Australia, New Zealand, and the Cocos Islands in the Indian Ocean. Here Darwin had the opportunity to study the formation of coral islands and reefs. Rounding the Horn of Africa in July 1836, the *Beagle* sailed north, reaching Falmouth, England, on October 2, 1836.

Darwin had returned from the five-year voyage with well-developed scientific skills and a vast amount of information. He also had many unanswered questions about the natural world and its inhabitants. Darwin would spend the next forty years of his life seeking answers to these questions.

This 1845 British naval map of the Galápagos Islands was based on charts drawn by Captain FitzRoy while on the *Beagle* expedition. The handwriting at the top is from a separate letter written and signed by FitzRoy.

This illustration of a Galápagos tortoise appeared in the first illustrated edition of Darwin's *Beagle* journals. It was published in 1890, after Darwin's death.

Chapter Two

BUILDING A
THEORY

Charles Darwin returned to a Great Britain that had changed during the five years of the *Beagle* voyage. New laws had extended the vote to more classes of British citizens, but there were still demands for increased representation. The growing number of poor people in British society were seeking relief from their situation. The Reform Bill of 1832 allowed the poor to receive aid only if they lived in public workhouses. The miserable conditions in these facilities were designed to discourage people from relying on public assistance and force them to get jobs. Middle-class factory owners supported this new law. Radical political leaders protested its harshness.

During this time of social change, most British citizens viewed radical movements and ideas of any kind with suspicion and fear. Charles Darwin had begun to develop some very radical ideas about the nature and meaning of life.

FIRST STEPS

After the *Beagle* adventure, Charles Darwin's planned career as a clergyman was forgotten. With the financial support of his father, he became a dedicated man of science. Darwin's first task after his return was dealing with all the specimens of animals, plants, and fossils that he had collected. He sought the help of friends and fellow scientists in making a catalog of this varied material. His friend John Henslow took on the job of organizing the plant specimens. Richard Owen, a professor of surgery and an expert in fossils, examined Darwin's fossil finds. Geologist Charles Lyell read and was impressed by Darwin's reports on the rocks and land formations of South America.

Darwin had asked John Gould, an expert on birds, to go over the thousands of birds specimens in the *Beagle* collection. When Gould examined the birds from the Galápagos Islands, he noticed something unusual. The thirteen kinds of Galápagos finches were similar to one another and to finches found in South America. Yet

Well-known geologist Charles Lyell *(facing page)* **was among the many professional friends and colleagues who helped Darwin organize and assess the specimens and information he brought back from his** *Beagle* **voyage.**

Gould noticed slight differences, particularly in the shape and size of their beaks. Darwin had also observed these differences but had not kept a record of which islands the finches had come from. He had, however, labeled the mockingbirds he had collected. Gould and Darwin realized that there were several distinct species of mockingbirds. Each came from a different island.

This discovery reminded Darwin of other things he had learned in the Galápagos Islands. He remembered being told that the giant tortoises on the different islands had slightly different shells. If these reports were true, perhaps the tortoises also represented different species. But why would these small islands, so close together and so similar, be inhabited by different kinds of creatures? Why would God have created so many variations on a few basic themes?

Darwin thought he might have the answer to these questions. Transmutation, Lamarck's theory of gradual change, could explain the distinct species of the Galápagos Islands. Finches or tortoises isolated on separate islands might have changed enough over time that they became completely different from one another and also from their ancestors. In his *Journal of Researches*, Darwin wrote, "Here, both in space and time, we seem to be brought somewhat near to that great fact—that mystery of mysteries—the first appearance of new beings on this earth."

Charles Darwin was determined to solve "that mystery of mysteries." He had the basic idea, but he needed to work out the details and look for evidence that would support his idea or prove it incorrect.

THINKING ABOUT TRANSMUTATION

Beginning in 1837, Charles Darwin recorded his ideas about transmutation in a series of notebooks. He had started using the so-called Red Notebook (it had a red cover) on the *Beagle* voyage and finished it back in England. Then followed Notebooks A through E. Two others were marked M and N.

> "All animals of same species are bound together just like buds of plants, which die at one time, though produced either sooner or later. Prove animals like plants—trace gradation between associated and non-associated animals—and the story will be complete."
>
> —Charles Darwin, Notebook B, 1837

These two pages in Darwin's writing are from one of the fourteen notebooks in which he recorded his observations during the *Beagle* voyage. When he returned to England, he continued the practice of recording in small notebooks his thinking about geology, transmutation, and other issues.

The material in the notebooks was not organized or carefully developed. Instead, it was a collection of random notes related in some way to transmutation.

Notebook A dealt mainly with geology. In the B and C notebooks, Darwin began to think about the way in which transmutation might take place. He knew that Lamarck had based his theory of change on the small variations that often existed among individuals in a single species. For example, one animal might be born with better eyesight or stronger teeth than its relatives. Darwin believed that this kind of variation was the key to the process by which species change.

The next step in the process was reproduction. If a male and a female with better eyesight happened to mate, they might pass on this same trait to their offspring. Darwin, like all scientists of his day, knew nothing about genes or the genetic process of sexual reproduction. He did know that traits from male and female parents somehow combined in their offspring. This could be seen in the breeding of domestic animals. Breeders of dogs, cattle, and sheep selected individuals with some desired characteristics such as longer tails or thicker wool. Then they mated these animals with each other. Repeated matings eventually produced a distinct breed very different from its ancestors.

Darwin learned as much as he could about plant and animal breeding by reading and talking to specialists. His C notebook included his notes on this important subject. He was especially fascinated by the many kinds of domestic pigeons, some with fantastic feathers and body shapes. Darwin's study of artificial breeding convinced him that a similar system of change based on variations took place in the natural world. But how did it work?

Human beings did the work of selecting specific variations when it came to animal breeding. Was there some supernatural being that controlled the process of selection in nature? Darwin doubted it. Then, while working on his D notebook in 1838, he found an answer to the puzzle. Natural selection was the force that made transmutation work.

Natural selection

Darwin developed the idea of natural selection after reading an important work published more than forty years earlier. It was *An Essay on the Principle of Population*, written by Thomas Malthus, a British clergyman.

In his essay, Malthus claimed that because of the "passion between the sexes," human populations usually continued to grow until they ran out of food. When this happened, sickness and starvation reduced the number of people to a level that matched the food supply. In Malthus's view, this was a natural and useful system. It prevented overpopulation. It also rewarded those who worked hard and didn't have too many children. The weak and lazy lost out because of their own behavior.

In his book, Malthus pictured the human race engaged in an unending competition over food and other resources. When Darwin read Malthus, he immediately saw how competition might be a factor in causing species to change.

If the food supply in a certain area was reduced by some natural disaster, members of a species in that area would have to compete with one another for food. Some individuals in the species might have been born with a special trait, for example, big, strong teeth. Because of this, they would be able to eat a wider variety of food than others in the species with smaller, weaker teeth. The big-teeth animals would survive, while others in the group died of starvation. When the survivors mated with each other, they would pass on the same big teeth that had made them so successful.

Animal breeders used artificial selection to reproduce desirable traits. In Darwin's theory, the impersonal forces of nature "selected" traits that enabled living things to survive. Other creatures without these favorable traits lost out in the competition over resources. In his book, Malthus had used the term *struggle for existence* to describe conflict between groups of people in central Asia. Darwin borrowed the phrase and applied it to all of nature.

TO MARRY OR NOT

Just as he analyzed scientific evidence, Darwin carefully examined the pros and cons of marriage. Writing on scraps of paper, he listed the options: "Not marry.... Freedom to go where one liked.... Conversation of clever men at clubs.... Not forced to visit relatives."

There were also advantages on the marriage side: "Children—(if it Please God)—Constant companion, (& friend in old age).... Home, & someone to take care of house.... These things good for one's health."

Charles and Emma Darwin married in 1839. The Darwins had ten children, two of which died when they were babies. This image of Emma and Leonard, the couple's eighth child, was taken when Leonard was about four years old.

MARRIAGE AND FAMILY

During 1838 Charles Darwin continued to work on the theory of natural selection, but he was also busy with other activities. He attended meetings of scientific groups such as the Zoological Society and the Geology Society, where he presented papers about the *Beagle* finds. He was also working on a book based on his *Beagle* journals. His life was full, but his health was suffering. Darwin decided that he needed the help of a wife.

In November 1838, Darwin proposed marriage to Emma Wedgwood, a close relative and longtime acquaintance. Emma was the daughter of Josiah Wedgwood II and Charles's first cousin. (His mother and Emma's father were brother and sister.) She was well educated, with domestic skills suited to running a household. The couple were married in January of the following year.

Emma Darwin was a religious woman who believed in the traditional doctrines of Christianity. Charles's views, on the other

hand, had become more and more
radical. Before they were married,
he felt it necessary to tell her about
his religious doubts. Emma was
concerned. In a letter to Charles, she
wrote of her fear "that our opinions
on the most important subject should
differ widely. My reason tells me
that honest & conscientious doubts
cannot be a sin, but I feel it would be
a painful void between us."

"LIKE CONFESSING A MURDER"

By the early 1840s, Charles Darwin had established the key ideas of
his theory. Variations existed among members of a species. Sexual
reproduction passed on variations from one generation to another.
Natural selection determined which variations would survive and
which would disappear. Darwin had a great deal of information
that supported his ideas. He wanted even more evidence before he
revealed his controversial theory to the world.

In 1842 the Darwins bought a comfortable house in the village
of Down, located about two hours from London. Here Charles,
Emma, and their two children, William and Anne, settled down
to a peaceful country life. Charles's life in science, however, was
anything but peaceful. He wrote hundreds of letters to friends
and acquaintances, asking for information that would further his
research. He also requested plant and animal specimens from
scientists traveling in distant lands. Among them was a young man
named Alfred Russel Wallace, who was on a collecting expedition
in Southeast Asia. Darwin asked him to send specimens of domestic
fowl from the region.

Darwin was also busy doing experiments to better understand
transmutation. He bred pigeons in the garden and raised plants in
a greenhouse. He also began a study of barnacles, using specimens

Darwin was in regular and frequent correspondence with prominent scientists of his time. Darwin wrote this postcard to Alfred Russel Wallace, a scientist who, like Darwin, came to believe in an evolutionary explanation for how and why species change.

BARNACLES

Darwin's children were so accustomed to their father's long research project on barnacles that they thought barnacles were part of every family's life. When young George Darwin visited the home of a schoolmate, he asked his friend, "Where does your father do *his* barnacles?"

collected on the *Beagle* voyage. This research, designed to show how species changed, stretched on for eight years. Darwin published several articles on his barnacle research but did not include anything about transmutation. The subject also was not mentioned in any of his many publications on the *Beagle* discoveries.

Darwin had begun to tell a few friends about the direction his research was taking. In letters and conversations, he mentioned to Lyell, Sedgwick, and others that he was working on a theory of transmutation. In 1844 he wrote to Leonard Jenyns, a friend from Cambridge. In the letter, Darwin gave a clear description of his work:

The general conclusion at which I have slowly been driven ... is that species are mutable & that allied species are co-descendants of common stocks. I know how much I open myself, to reproach, for such a conclusion, but I have at least honestly & deliberately come to it.

That same year, Darwin gave a similar account of his research in a letter to Joseph Hooker, a young botanist. The admission, Darwin said, was "like confessing a murder."

In 1844 Darwin had particular reason to believe that his ideas might open him to extreme reproach. A recently published book called *Vestiges of the Natural History of Creation* had put the topics of transmutation into the public spotlight. The author, who did not reveal his name, had written about a variety of sensational subjects. Among them were the origin of life and the descent of humans from animal ancestors.

"Mr. Vestiges," as he was known, was no scientist. He was a popular writer who presented a collection of miscellaneous "facts" to support his ideas. His book was a popular success and was read by many people. Most scientists, however, criticized *Vestiges* for its inaccuracies. Church leaders were disturbed by the book's antireligious nature. The reception of *Vestiges* convinced Darwin that his own ideas about transmutation were not ready to be presented to the world.

Chapter Three

ON THE ORIGIN OF SPECIES

By the mid-1840s, Charles Darwin had spent more than ten years working on his theory of transmutation. Though not ready to publish his work, he wrote a 230-page essay in 1844 outlining his basic ideas. He then began writing "Natural Selection," a longer, more detailed manuscript presenting his theory. He also continued working on his never-ending barnacle project. In 1851 the Darwin family was struck by tragedy when Charles and Emma's ten-year-old daughter, Annie, died of scarlet fever. During this period, Charles himself was again suffering from ill health, with spells of vomiting and severe headaches almost daily.

Despite his grief and illness, Darwin never stopped writing. The chapters of his "big book" slowly piled up. Then, in June 1858, everything changed.

LETTER FROM TERNATE

Around June 18, Darwin received a thick envelope. It had been mailed from Ternate, an island in the Malay Archipelago (present-day Indonesia). The name on the

This photo of Anne Darwin, said to be Charles's favorite child, was taken in 1849, the year she came down with scarlet fever. She died in 1851, not long after her tenth birthday.

ALFRED RUSSEL WALLACE

Alfred Russel Wallace (1823–1913) came from a poor family and had to work for a living. He was a commercial collector of animal and plant specimens for museums and wealthy clients. While collecting in the Malay Archipelago during the 1840s, he developed a theory of evolution very similar to Charles Darwin's. After his return to England, Wallace became a loyal friend and supporter of Darwin. In his later years, he disagreed with Darwin over the subject of human evolution.

Alfred Russel Wallace was not only a prominent man of science but also a spokesman for radical causes. He supported women's voting rights and land reform favoring the average person over the wealthy.

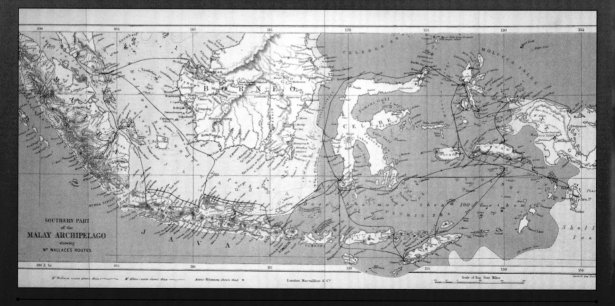

Alfred Russel Wallace kept notes during his expedition to the Malay Archipelago. This page shows his drawing of a hornbill, including notes about the color of its head (red, blue, and black) and beak (orange) and its diet (fruit and insects).

Wallace created this map of the Malay Archipelago. This region of Southeast Asia includes thousands of islands, including those of Indonesia and the Philippines.

envelope was Alfred Russel Wallace, the young collector from whom Darwin had earlier requested bird specimens. Wallace was only one of Darwin's hundreds of correspondents, and not a very important one. Darwin opened his letter with little anticipation. What he found was so deeply shocking that it changed the course of his life.

Enclosed with Wallace's letter was a twenty-page manuscript titled "On the Tendency of Varieties to Depart Indefinitely from the Original Type." As Darwin read it, he realized that Wallace had come up with a theory of transmutation that was almost the same as his own. It even included a version of natural selection. Darwin was astonished and horrified. All his years of hard work and someone else had gotten there ahead of him.

In his letter, Wallace asked Darwin if he would kindly forward the manuscript to the great scientist Charles Lyell, Darwin's good friend. Darwin did as requested. He pointed out the "striking coincidence" between his ideas and Wallace's and asked for Lyell's advice. Darwin wrote, "I should be extremely glad now to publish a sketch of my general views in about a dozen pages or so. But I cannot persuade myself that I can do so honourably." Darwin did not want to claim another person's ideas as

JOSEPH DALTON HOOKER

Joseph Dalton Hooker (1817–1911) was a famous botanist and world traveler. During his long career, he made expeditions to the Antarctic region, Morocco, and the United States. In the early 1840s, Hooker *(below)* assisted Darwin with botanical research and became his close friend and adviser. In Hooker's own career as a botanist, he served for twenty years as director of Britain's Royal Botanic Garden in London.

his own. He could not bear that Wallace or any man "should think that I had behaved in a paltry [small-minded] spirit."

Lyell's response was swift and reassuring. Of course, Wallace's manuscript could not be ignored. But this did not mean that Darwin should put aside his own work. After consulting with Joseph Hooker, Lyell came up with a plan. They would arrange for a joint publication of Darwin's and Wallace's ideas. This would take the form of a paper to be presented before a scientific society.

Hooker and Lyell chose a meeting of the Linnean Society in London as the occasion for the momentous announcement. On June 31, 1858, the society secretary read aloud Wallace's paper along with passages from Darwin's 1844 essay on transmutation. Also included in the reading were parts of a letter that Darwin had written to a friend describing his theory. Darwin himself did not attend the meeting. He was in mourning for his infant son Charles, the Darwins' tenth child, who had died only a few days earlier. Wallace, far away in the Malay Archipelago, was informed of the event in a letter that would not reach him for at least four months. His approval had not been requested.

"ONE LONG ARGUMENT"

After the presentation at the Linnean Society, Darwin was ready to publish his ideas in a book. It would not be a long, scholarly volume. Instead, it would be a shorter work addressed to a general audience of well-educated readers.

Encouraged by his friends, Darwin began working on the book. He took material from the "Natural Selection" manuscript and rewrote it in a simpler form. He also added information from his notebooks and other records of his research. His ceaseless efforts affected his health, and he again experienced periods of vomiting. Darwin wrote to Hooker, saying "My God how I long for my stomach's sake to wash my hands of it." In another letter to his cousin William Fox, he wrote, "So much for my abominable volume, which has cost me so much labour that I almost hate it."

Darwin wrote the book as "one long argument" that would explain and support his theory of transmutation by means of natural selection. In the first few chapters, he described his research on artificial breeding and Malthus's ideas about competition over resources. Then in the fourth chapter, Darwin presented his own theory of natural selection. He argued,

> *If [variations] do occur, can we doubt (remembering that many more individuals are born than can possibly survive) that individuals having any advantage, however slight, over others, would have the best chance of surviving and of procreating their kind? . . . . This preservation of favourable variations, and the rejection of injurious variations, I have called Natural Selection.*

Darwin wrote several other chapters showing how his theory could be applied in different areas of science such as geology and paleontology. He even included two chapters discussing the

"Long before having arrived at this part of my work, a crowd of difficulties will have occurred to the reader. Some of them are so grave that . . . I can never reflect on them without being staggered, but, to the best of my judgment, the greater number are only apparent, and those that are real are not, I think, fatal to the theory."

—**Charles Darwin**, *On the Origin of Species*, **1859**

EVOLUTION OF TERMS

In the last paragraph of *On the Origin of Species,* Darwin spoke of natural forms "evolving," but he did not use the term *evolution* in the book. The words he used most often to describe his theory were "descent with modification." It would not be until many years later that *evolution* became the accepted term for Darwin's theory.

From the Author

original issue in original green cloth COS

1859
1250 Copies published all sold the first day

19 JUN 1926

ON

THE ORIGIN OF SPECIES

BY MEANS OF NATURAL SELECTION,

OR THE

PRESERVATION OF FAVOURED RACES IN THE STRUGGLE
FOR LIFE.

By CHARLES DARWIN, M.A.,

FELLOW OF THE ROYAL, GEOLOGICAL, LINNÆAN, ETC., SOCIETIES;
AUTHOR OF 'JOURNAL OF RESEARCHES DURING H. M. S. BEAGLE'S VOYAGE
ROUND THE WORLD.'

LONDON:
JOHN MURRAY, ALBEMARLE STREET.
1859.

The right of Translation is reserved.

The full title of Darwin's groundbreaking 1859 book was *On the Origin of Species by Means of Natural Selection, or the Preservation of Favoured Races in the Struggle for Life.* **This is a photo of the title page of the first edition of the work.**

difficulty of the theory and possible objections to it. He ended the book with an eloquent statement of his beliefs:

> *It is interesting to contemplate a tangled bank, clothed with many plants of many kinds, with birds singing on the bushes, with various insects flitting about,...and to reflect that these elaborately constructed forms, so different from each other,...have all been produced by laws acting around us....There is a grandeur to this view of life, with its several powers, having been originally breathed into a few forms or into one; and that whilst this planet has gone cycling on according to the fixed law of gravity, from so simple a beginning endless forms most beautiful and most wonderful have been, and are being evolved.*

ON THE ORIGIN OF SPECIES

After months of feverish work, Darwin finished writing his book in May 1859. He had signed a contract with a well-known publisher, John Murray, who had issued the second edition of Darwin's *Journal of Researches*. Murray was eager to publish this new work by the famous naturalist of the *Beagle* voyage.

Murray suggested calling the book *On the Origin of Species by Means of Natural Selection, or the Preservation of Favoured Races in the Struggle for Life*. This was the title on the green cloth cover when the book was published on November 24, 1859. Darwin's "abominable volume" was finally in the hands of the reading public. The author waited for the storm that he was sure would follow.

Chapter Four

THE
CONTROVERSY
BEGINS

The publication of *The Origin of Species* aroused controversy for a number of reasons. Some readers condemned Darwin's ideas on religious grounds. Others disagreed with details of the scientific theory. Some critics combined religious and scientific objections. For many readers, Darwin's book raised questions about the nature and meaning of life that were deeply disturbing.

FIRST REACTIONS

As Darwin had feared, the first comments on *The Origin of Species* were unfavorable. They appeared even before the book had reached the bookstores. An influential magazine, the *Athenaeum*, had gotten an advance copy of the book and published an anonymous review. The reviewer's comments were hostile and full of sarcasm. "We cannot pretend," he said, "to follow our author in his wanderings through the whole series of phenomena associated with his subject. He omits nothing, and he fears nothing."

Darwin's friends were quick to send letters of congratulations and praise. Charles Lyell praised *Origin* as "a splendid case of close reasoning & long sustained argument." Joseph Hooker told Darwin, "I would rather be the author of your book than of any other on natural history science."

A new friend, the zoologist Thomas Henry Huxley, was also delighted by the book. Although he did not agree with all of Darwin's

THOMAS HENRY HUXLEY

Thomas Henry Huxley (1825–1895) was one of Charles Darwin's most enthusiastic supporters. Huxley *(facing page)* began his career as an assistant surgeon on a navy ship charting the seas around Australia. During the voyage, he did research on marine organisms. After returning to England in 1850, he earned a living by lecturing and writing popular articles on science. Huxley had a long-standing dispute with Richard Owen about the connection between humans and apes.

ideas, he supported the theory as a whole. Huxley wrote an anonymous review for a popular London newspaper, the *Times*. He gave a detailed account of the book and praised Darwin's contributions to the advancement of science.

Darwin had sent a copy of his book to Alfred Russel Wallace, who was still in Southeast Asia on a collecting trip. Wallace expressed high praise for Darwin's book. He told a friend, "I really feel thankful that it has not been left to me to give the theory to the world."

Not all of Darwin's friends were pleased by the publication of *The Origin of Species*. His old geology teacher, Adam Sedgwick, was shocked by the ideas in the book. "I have read your book with more pain than pleasure," he wrote Darwin. Sedgwick considered some of Darwin's ideas to be "utterly false & grievously mischievous." He accused Darwin of destroying religious values.

Richard Owen, another old colleague of Darwin's, also was not happy with his book. When Darwin visited him at his home, Owen criticized *The Origin of Species* for its controversial ideas. He later attacked the book in a review published in an Edinburgh newspaper.

ASA GRAY

Asa Gray (1810–1888) was a professor of natural history at Harvard University in Cambridge, Massachusetts. Although he and Darwin met several times in England, they communicated mainly by letter. Gray arranged for the first U.S. publication of *On the Origin of Species* in 1860. He wrote reviews and articles about Darwin's theory and defended it against the attacks of his influential Harvard colleague Louis Agassiz (1807–1873). Agassiz rejected evolution because it went against his religious beliefs.

DARWIN'S SUPPORTERS

Because of his poor health and sensitive nerves, Charles Darwin disliked public controversy. His supporters were more than happy to speak out in defense of his theory. Darwin's defense team was made up of scientists whose own research had led them in similar directions. They included geologist Charles Lyell, botanist Joseph Hooker, zoologist Thomas Henry Huxley, and botanist Asa Gray. The first three did their work in Great Britain. Gray, a professor of natural history at Harvard University in Massachusetts, represented Darwin's views in the world of American science.

These men wrote reviews, articles, and books. They gave speeches and argued with friends and enemies, all in defense of Darwin's theory of evolution. Although the four did not agree with every point, they believed that Darwin's ideas would bring about a revolution in science.

While Darwin did not play a public role in defending his theory, he was active behind the scenes. He wrote hundreds of letters promoting his book and urging friends and acquaintances to support it.

CONFRONTATION IN OXFORD

One of the most famous confrontations between Darwin's supporters and those opposed to his theory took place in June 1860. The event was the annual meeting of the British Association for the Advancement of Science, held at Oxford University. The weeklong meeting was attended by many who had read Darwin's book and wanted to discuss his ideas. Darwin himself was not there, but Joseph Hooker and Thomas Huxley were. Also in attendance was Richard Owen, who had already expressed his disapproval of Darwin's theory. An important clergyman, Samuel Wilberforce, the bishop of Oxford, was also present.

At the meeting, Richard Owen spoke out against the idea that humans had descended from apes or other animals. (In *Origin*, Darwin had said that all animals had probably descended from just a few ancestors, but he never mentioned apes.) Owen insisted that the differences between the brains of humans and apes made any relationship between them impossible. Huxley replied that the differences were not important. He believed that apes and humans

Among the many people who disagreed with Darwin's theory of evolution were members of the church establishment. One of the most powerful voices of opposition was that of Samuel Wilberforce *(below)*, a bishop in the Church of England.

This page from Darwin's B notebook (from around 1837) shows his first sketch of an evolutionary tree. The scientific tree of life shows the relationships among species and their ancestors. Darwin's idea that all animals—including humans—were descended from common ancestors caused public outrage.

were very likely related. As the meeting progressed, the subject of apes and humans came up in many speeches. Finally, Bishop Samuel Wilberforce took the stage.

Wilberforce was a powerful church leader who also had influence in the world of science. He was known as Soapy Sam to his enemies because of his smooth style of speaking. Addressing the crowd at the British Association for the Advancement of Science meeting, Wilberforce said that facts did not support Darwin's theory of evolution. In the bishop's view, humans were distinctly different from other animals, including apes. At some point in his speech, Wilberforce turned his attention to Thomas Huxley. In a sarcastic tone, he asked whether Huxley was related to an ape on his grandfather's or grandmother's side of the family.

Huxley, who considered himself "Darwin's bulldog," was ready with his response. He vigorously pointed out the errors in Wilberforce's argument and praised the logic of Darwin's theory. In his final words, Huxley delivered a devastating attack on the bishop:

If I would rather have a miserable ape for a grandfather or a man highly endowed by nature and possessed of great means and influence, and yet who employs those faculties for the mere purpose of introducing ridicule into a grave scientific discussion—I unhesitatingly affirm my preference for the ape.

DIFFERING ACCOUNTS

Joseph Hooker's account of the confrontation in Oxford was not quite the same as Thomas Huxley's. In a letter to Darwin, Hooker suggested that he himself was the one who led the attack on the bishop. He gave a speech proving that Wilberforce had not even read *On the Origin of Species.* "Sam was shut up—had not one word to say in reply," Hooker reported.

For Darwin's supporters, the events at the British Association for the Advancement of Science meeting represented a clear victory for their side. They had challenged the church and the scientific establishment, and they had won. Yet Bishop Wilberforce and his followers believed that their point of view had triumphed. The meeting at Oxford was only the first of many confrontations between the two opposing sides.

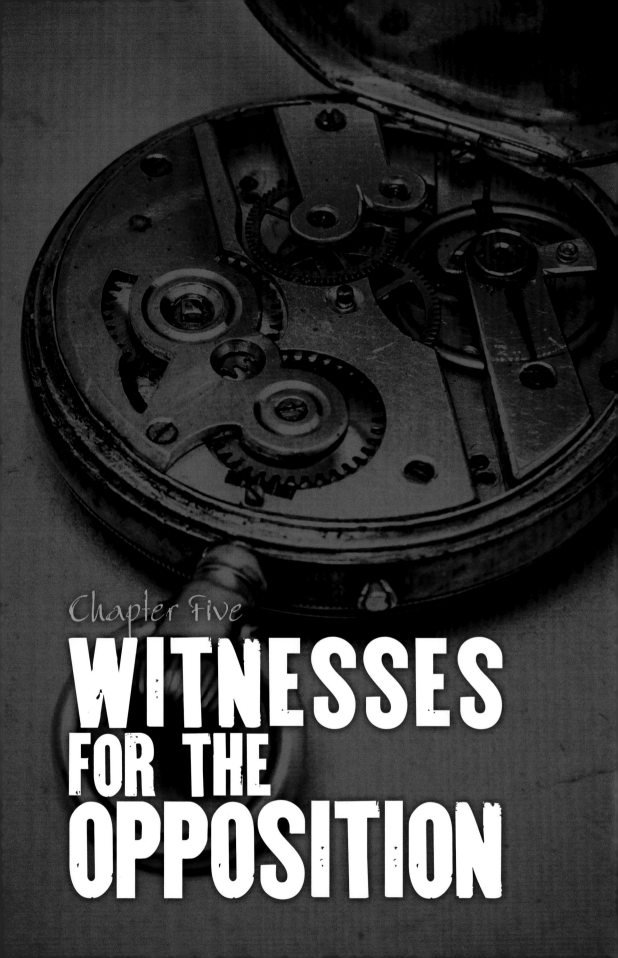

Chapter Five

WITNESSES FOR THE OPPOSITION

Those who opposed Darwin and his theory were not as well organized as his famous defense team. Bishop Wilberforce and other religious leaders made speeches and wrote articles, but they did not plan their attacks. Nevertheless, they found many opportunities to express their disagreement.

RELIGIOUS OBJECTIONS

Darwin's theory of the origin of species was generally seen as an attack on the Christian religion. This was not because it contradicted the story of creation in the Bible. By the mid-1800s, many educated people in Britain, Europe, and the United States had begun to view the Genesis story in a new way. They saw it not as an actual account of creation but as a story symbolizing God's power. All the same, faithful Christians and even people with liberal religious beliefs were profoundly shocked that God seemed to have no role in the world Darwin envisioned.

At this time, many religious thinkers accepted the idea of natural theology. The chief proponent of natural theology was a British clergyman named William Paley, who had written an influential book published in 1802. Paley saw God not as the hands-on Creator of the Genesis story. Instead, God was a divine authority who set the world in motion and established natural laws that kept it running.

As proof of God's existence and role in creation, Paley pointed to the evidence of design in the world. He used the image of a watch to demonstrate his point. He wrote that when we examine the complex mechanism of a watch, we understand that it has been made for a specific purpose. From that, we assume that some individual or being designed the watch. Similarly, Paley reasoned that all the complex elements of the natural world represent the work of a divine designer, God.

In Darwin's theory, the intricate forms of natural organisms

William Paley was an influential philosopher. In his famous book *Natural Theology* **(1802), he argued that a watch's complex design** *(facing page)* **requires the existence of a designer. In the same way, he believed the complexity of life proved the existence of God.**

illustrate not the work of God but of natural selection. It is this force that creates complex beings by selecting and combining random variations. Darwin's theory does not rely on a vision of grand design with a divine designer.

The idea of a world with no divine plan or purpose was unthinkable to many, including some of Darwin's friends and supporters. Asa Gray, Darwin's defender in the United States, was one of these. Gray tried to find a middle ground between Darwin's ideas and his own strong religious beliefs. Perhaps God had created the variations among individuals, and the forces of natural selection then operated on these variations. Darwin wrote to Gray, saying "I cannot think that the world, as we see it, is the result of chance; & yet I cannot look at each separate thing as the result of design."

Darwin's uncertain views on divine design in the universe eventually led him to make changes in *The Origin of Species.* In the second edition of the book, he added the notion of a creator to the final paragraph: "There is a grandeur to this view of life, with its several powers, having been originally breathed by the Creator into a few forms or many. . . ."

Darwin later said that he made this change because he felt pressured by his friends and by public opinion. When he wrote his autobiography in 1876, he included a final word on the question of divine design.

> *The old argument of design in nature . . . fails, now that the law of natural selection has been discovered. . . . There seems to be no more design in the variability of organic beings and in the action of natural selection, than in the course by which the wind blows.*

Apes and humans

Many of those who opposed Darwin's ideas were concerned by one specific aspect of his theory: the origin of humans. In *The Origin of Species,* Darwin had said almost nothing about this subject.

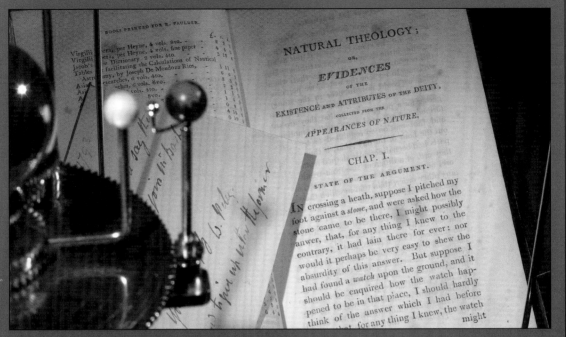

Darwin admired Paley's watchmaker analogy but came to a very different explanation for the complexity of life on Earth. This image shows original published text from Paley's *Natural Theology* in which he makes the famous comparison.

"The marks of design are too strong to be got over. Design must have had a designer. That designer must have been a person. That person is GOD."

—**William Paley**, *Natural Theology*, **1802**

Asa Gray (*pictured*) was a highly influential American botanist in the 1800s. He helped arrange for the 1860 publication of Darwin's *Origin* in the United States.

HUMAN ORIGINS

The only specific reference to the subject of human origins in *On the Origin of Species* comes in the concluding chapter. Darwin wrote, "In the future I see open fields for far more important researches.... Much light will be thrown on the origin of man and his history."

His readers, however, believed the implications of his theory were clear. Darwin was claiming that humans had evolved from animals such as apes.

According to traditional Christian teachings, humans are basically different from other animals because they have minds and souls. These God-given gifts separate the human race from all other living beings. How could humans have evolved from apes or other "lower" animals that lacked these attributes?

In the mid-1800s, the British were fascinated by accounts of gorillas and other apes brought back by European explorers in Asia and Africa. The public saw its first live ape in 1837 when Jenny the orangutan was put on display at the London Zoo. Richard Owen and other scientists were also interested in apes. As a result, many of the arguments over Darwin's theory focused on the ape issue. Were humans descended from gorillas, chimpanzees, and other apes or even from monkeys? Newspapers and magazines published cartoons showing apes dressed in human clothing. Darwin himself was often pictured with his head atop an ape's body. Thomas Huxley contributed to the craze by presenting a series of popular lectures about the ape-human connection.

Darwin did not join in the public argument about humans descending from apes. He did attempt to answer the question of whether humans differed from apes and other animals because of their minds or souls. His book *The Descent of Man*, published in 1871, dealt with this sensitive subject. In it, Darwin tried to show how human intelligence, language, and moral sense could have been the products of evolution. His critics and even his closest supporters were not convinced. This issue would be part of the evolution debate for many years.

QUESTIONS ABOUT NATURAL SELECTION

Some of the objections to Darwin's theory came from other scientists. During the 1860s and the 1870s, many scientists

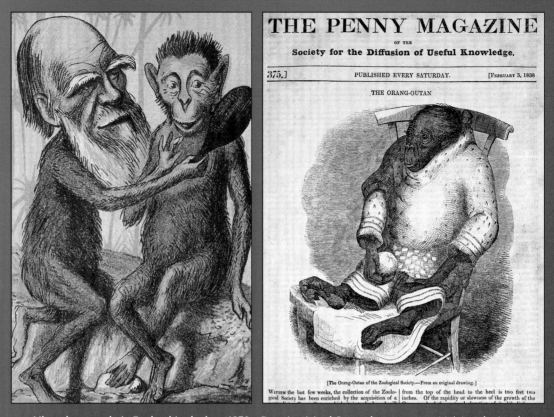

THE PENNY MAGAZINE
OF THE
Society for the Diffusion of Useful Knowledge.

375.]   PUBLISHED EVERY SATURDAY.   [FEBRUARY 3, 1838

THE ORANG-OUTAN

[The Orang-Outan of the Zoological Society.—From an original drawing.]

WITHIN the last few weeks, the collection of the Zoological Society has been enriched by the acquisition of a | from the top of the head to the heel is two feet two inches. Of the rapidity or slowness of the growth of the

Like other people in England in the late 1830s, Darwin visited Jenny the orangutan *(right)* at the London Zoo. He was struck by her intelligence and emotional depth, writing that humans were perhaps not as superior to such animals as they would like to think. Darwin's controversial theory of evolution made him a target of public ridicule. He was often shown with his head on an apelike body, as in this British caricature *(left)* from 1874.

THE

DESCENT OF MAN,

AND

SELECTION IN RELATION TO SEX.

BY CHARLES DARWIN, M.A., F.R.S., &c.

IN TWO VOLUMES.—VOL. II.

WITH ILLUSTRATIONS.

LONDON:
JOHN MURRAY, ALBEMARLE STREET.
1871.

HUMAN ORIGINS

Robert FitzRoy, captain of the *Beagle,* wrote to a friend about Darwin's theory of evolution: "I, at least, *cannot* find anything 'ennobling' in the thought of being a descendant of even the *most* ancient Ape."

Darwin's *The Descent of Man* was first published in 1871. It was later translated into many other languages, including German, Russian, and French.

accepted the basic idea that species evolve from other species. They were not convinced, however, that natural selection was the force that made evolution work.

Some were put off by the idea of a continual struggle for existence among living things. Others questioned the random variations among individuals that provided the raw material for natural selection. Where did these variations come from? Were they truly random? Or was there some law that controlled their existence?

In *The Origin of Species*, Darwin had attempted to explain the existence of random variations. He finally had to admit, "Our ignorance of the laws of variation is profound. Not in one case out of a hundred can we pretend to assign any reason why this or that part differs...from the same part in the parents." In 1868 he tackled the subject again in another book, *On the Variations of Animals and Plants Under Domestication*. Darwin was still not sure about the origins of variations. (This knowledge would not be possible until the development of modern genetic theory in the 1900s). He believed, however, that he could explain how variations were inherited.

At that time, most scientists believed in blended inheritance. They thought that the traits of parents blended together during reproduction. For example, if one human parent was very tall and the other very short, their children should all be of medium height. Some of Darwin's critics claimed that blended inheritance made the passing on of favorable variations impossible. Unless both parents happened to have exactly the same traits, any distinctive variations would be diluted or lost in the blending process.

Darwin accepted the general idea of blended inheritance, but he came up with an additional concept that fit better with the process of natural selection. He called his new idea pangenesis. According to this theory, the bodies of all living organisms produce tiny particles, called gemmules, that make inheritance possible. Every kind of organ, tissue, and body part produces specific gemmules that contain information about its own nature and function. All the gemmules in an organism are carried to the reproductive organs by the blood stream. In the process of reproduction, they are passed on to the next generation. Each new being inherits a unique combination of these units of inheritance.

Darwin did not have much solid information to back up his theory of pangenesis. Other scientists who were trying to understand heredity at the time were in the same position. There was one exception. An Austrian monk named Gregor Mendel was experimenting with the actual process of inheritance.

Mendel did his famous experiments with pea plants in the 1860s. He wrote a paper describing his work, which was published in the journal of a local natural history society in 1865. Mendel also sent his article to a few scientists, but no one seemed to have noticed. If Darwin and other researchers had known of Mendel's experiments, their understanding of heredity would have been greatly increased. Mendel's groundbreaking work would not be rediscovered for more than thirty years.

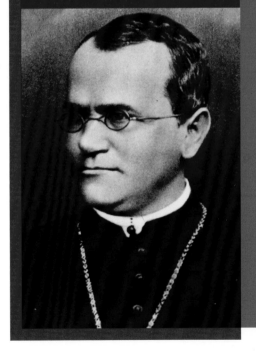

GREGOR MENDEL

Gregor Mendel (1822–1884) joined the Augustinian order in 1843 and entered a monastery in the town of Brno, located in the present-day Czech Republic. He studied science at the University of Vienna and then returned to the monastery in 1853 to teach high school science classes. He also spent many hours experimenting with garden peas. In 1868 Gregor Mendel *(below)* became abbot of the monastery and gave up his experiments.

Chapter Six

THE DECLINE
OF DARWINISM

When the extent of [Darwin's] work is properly estimated, it is not too much to say that among all the great leaders of human thought that have ever lived there are not half a dozen who have achieved as much as he.... [Darwin] has already found his place in the history of science by the side of Aristotle, Descartes, and Newton.

—J. Fiske, obituary in the *Atlantic Monthly,* **June 1882**

Charles Darwin died on April 19, 1882, at the age of seventy-three. He had spent the last years of his life at his home in Down working quietly on experiments in the garden and greenhouse. His final book, published the year before his death, was about earthworms. Although the arguments over evolution continued, Darwin was no longer actively involved in defending his theory.

During the later years of his life, Darwin had become an honored public figure in Great Britain. He was buried in Westminster Abbey in London, the same hallowed spot where British monarchs and famous poets are entombed. The man whose ideas had challenged some of the basic beliefs of religion had his final resting place in a church.

NATURAL SELECTION REJECTED

By the end of the 1800s, the majority of scientists in Britain, Europe, and the United States had rejected large parts of Darwin's theory. Most scientists accepted the basic idea of evolution: living things evolve from earlier forms of life. They had serious doubts, however, about natural selection as the force that made evolution work.

For natural selection to operate in the way that Darwin had described, Earth had to be many millions of years old. The gradual changes produced by natural selection required an

This photo of Darwin was taken in 1880 by Arnold Patrick Spencer-Smith (1883–1916). Spencer-Smith was an amateur British photographer who later crossed the seas of Antarctica on the *Endurance* with the famed Shackleton expedition of 1914–1917.

Down House, the home of Charles Darwin, is a major tourist attraction in southeastern England. Visitors can see the study *(above)* where Darwin wrote *On the Origin of Species*.

WILLIAM THOMSON

William Thomson (1824–1907) was an influential scientist who was given the title Lord Kelvin in recognition of his work. In addition to his pioneering research in thermodynamics, Thomson also contributed to the development of a new temperature scale. In this scale, absolute zero (−273°C or −459°F) is the lowest point. Still in use, the scale is called the Kelvin scale in his honor.

"incomprehensively vast" span of time to create new and different beings. In 1868 Scottish physicist William Thomson wrote a paper claiming that Earth was only 100 million years old. This would not allow enough time for the changes described in Darwin's theory.

Thomson based his claim on the new science of thermodynamics, which dealt with the nature of energy and heat. According to the principles of thermodynamics, heat at the core of Earth was cooling off at a predictable rate. Based on this rate, scientists could estimate the age of the planet. After issuing his first estimate, Thomson came up with new numbers that lowered Earth's age to as little as 10 million years. Later discoveries about radioactivity would prove that Thomson's figures were wrong. In the late 1800s, however, many scientists believed that they proved natural selection simply did not work.

THE REBIRTH OF LAMARCKISM

Many people who rejected natural selection turned to old ideas to explain evolution. These included the transmutation theory of Jean-Baptiste Lamarck. Scientists concentrated on two parts of Lamarck's theory: the law of use and disuse, and the inheritance of acquired characteristics.

Lamarck had claimed that a living being's organs and body parts could be strengthened and enlarged by continuous use. If these features were not used, they would eventually wither away and disappear. Lamarck's theory of the inheritance of acquired characteristics suggested that new traits developed through use could be passed on to the next generation. If a man developed very strong muscles because of the work he did, his children would be born with the same strong muscles. A giraffe that stretched its neck to reach the leaves on tall trees would have descendants with long necks.

In certain environments, long necks and strong muscles could prove to be an advantage. They would help in finding food or defeating enemies. Those who possessed these traits would survive and reproduce while others died. This process would gradually lead to the appearance of new species, just as natural selection did.

The difference was that in Lamarck's theory, favorable traits such as long necks or strong muscles could be produced by the actions of individuals. According to Darwin's theory of natural selection, such traits or variations occurred randomly. They were not affected by individual behavior. But the idea of random variations was the part of his theory that most scientists had rejected. By the late 1800s, many finally came to believe that Lamarck's theory provided a better mechanism for evolution. Even Darwin in his later years began to wonder if Lamarck had been at least partially right. In later editions of *Origin*, he added some of Lamarck's ideas about inheritance to the discussion of natural selection.

THE TIDE BEGINS TO TURN

In the late 1800s, discoveries in the new field of genetics brought renewed attention to Darwin's work. They would provide answers to questions that had puzzled scientists since *The Origin of Species* was first published in 1859. One of the first breaks came in the 1890s, when German scientist August Weismann developed a new theory of heredity based on his study of cells. He discovered a material in the cell's nucleus that he called germ plasm. This material made it possible for the characteristics of parents to be passed on during reproduction. It could not be affected by any changes that took place during an individual's lifetime.

Weismann's germ plasm theory of heredity contradicted Lamarck's belief that acquired characteristics could be inherited. In fact, Weismann claimed that his laboratory experiments on heredity proved Lamarck was wrong. Darwin's theory of natural selection was the correct explanation for evolutionary change. Many scientists disagreed with his conclusions and continued to support Lamarckian views. They would soon be forced to reconsider their position.

The major turning point leading to the revival of Darwin's theory was the rediscovery of Gregor Mendel's

TAILLESS RATS

August Weismann tested Lamarck's theory in an experiment using laboratory rats. He cut off the tails of a group of rats and then mated members of the group to each other. The offspring of the tailless rats were born with complete tails, just like normal rats. Weismann then cut off the tails of the second group of rats and repeated the experiment. There were still no tailless rats. No matter how many times the process was repeated, the rats continued to be born with tails.

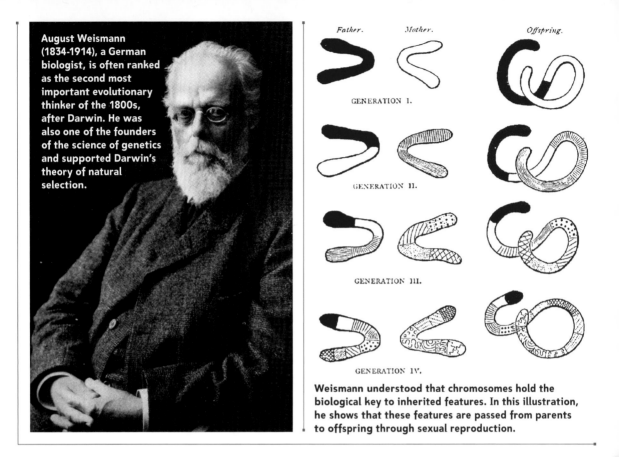

August Weismann (1834-1914), a German biologist, is often ranked as the second most important evolutionary thinker of the 1800s, after Darwin. He was also one of the founders of the science of genetics and supported Darwin's theory of natural selection.

Father.   Mother.   Offspring.

GENERATION I.

GENERATION II.

GENERATION III.

GENERATION IV.

Weismann understood that chromosomes hold the biological key to inherited features. In this illustration, he shows that these features are passed from parents to offspring through sexual reproduction.

pioneering work in genetics. Mendel did his experiments with pea plants in the 1860s, but his research had gone unnoticed until 1900. In that year, several scientists who were studying heredity in plants came across the article that Mendel had written in 1865.

Dutch botanist Hugo de Vries realized that Mendel's experiments helped to explain the results that he had found in his own work. In sexual reproduction, traits were passed on from parents to offspring by means of individual particles or units of inheritance. A new plant or animal received one set of these particles (now known as genes) from each parent. Instead of blending, the particles remained separate, forming new and different combinations in each offspring.

In his experiments, Mendel studied plant characteristics such as seed color that were controlled by a single gene. Later research would show that most inherited traits depend on more than one gene. The laws of inheritance were much more complicated than Mendel had suspected, but his work had prepared the way for the development of modern genetic theory.

Spencer used it in his own writings, along with Lamarckism. It was Spencer who originated the phrase "survival of the fittest" to describe natural selection. (At Thomas Huxley's urging, Darwin added the phrase to later editions of *Origin*.) Spencer also made the term *evolution* popular by using it frequently in his writings.

Herbert Spencer believed the same laws that controlled evolution in nature also applied to human society. Competition between individuals and businesses was natural and useful. In this struggle, the fittest—those who were strong and had superior abilities—would always survive. Their success and the elimination of their weaker rivals would create a more productive economic system. This would benefit society as a whole.

The "survival of the fittest" idea was also applied in world politics. During the 1800s, Great Britain and other European powers were expanding their empires. Government officials used the idea of natural selection to justify the rule of powerful nations over weaker ones. This argument was partially based on beliefs about differences among racial groups. According to the common view, the native peoples of Africa, Asia, and Australia were members of inferior races. They were less fit than white Europeans and unable to compete with them. Therefore, European dominance was not only just but also natural.

In the United States, politicians and social philosophers used these same ideas to justify the harsh treatment of Native Americans. These ideas were also called on to support discriminatory laws against former slaves after the Civil War (1861–1865).

THE EUGENICS MOVEMENT

Another element of Social Darwinism was the eugenics movement of the early 1900s. The term *eugenics* was coined in 1883 by Francis Galton, a British scientist and half cousin of Charles Darwin. Galton believed that natural selection should ideally produce human beings who were physically and mentally fit. Modern societies, however, often prevented this from happening by interfering in the natural course of events. People who were weak, sick, or mentally ill received aid from charities or from public health programs. These "unfit" individuals survived and produced offspring with the same unfavorable characteristics.

Francis Galton and other scientists who supported eugenics believed that steps should be taken to keep the human race healthy. They wanted to encourage the "fittest" members of society to have many children. The "unfit" should be discouraged from reproducing. In the view of most eugenicists, the fittest people were usually well-educated members of the middle class. The unfit were most often the lower classes, people of color, the poor, and those with mental disabilities.

In the late 1800s and the early decades of the 1900s, the eugenics movement became widespread in Britain, Europe, and the United States. In 1912 the first International Eugenics Congress was held in London, bringing together many supporters of the movement. Governments took up the cause of eugenics and set up agencies to identify unfit members of society. Those considered unfit included the mentally ill or people with diseases such as epilepsy. In Britain the Mental Deficiency Act of 1913 allowed for mentally impaired people to be put into asylums, where they were not allowed to have children.

In the United States, the Eugenics Record Office was created in 1910 to identify and locate people suffering from inherited mental illness. Around the same time, physician Henry Goddard developed a system of intelligence testing. He set up categories of mental impairment such as "feeble-minded," "moron," and "imbecile." Goddard recommended that people with such disorders be put permanently in institutions.

"The millionaires are a product of natural selection acting on the whole body of men to pick out those who can meet the requirement of certain work to be done.... It is because they are thus selected that wealth ... aggregates [collects] in their hands.... They get high wages and live in luxury, but the bargain is a good one for society."

—William Graham Sumner, American Social Darwinist, 1914

Social Darwinism also gave birth to the eugenics movement. In the United States, eugenics supporters sponsored Better Baby and Fitter Family competitions at state fairs such as this one in Kansas during the first half of the 1900s. Babies and families were judged on size, attractiveness, health, personality, and mental qualities. Prizes included bronze medals and champion cups.

Supporters of eugenics in Germany in the first half of the 1900s included scientists, doctors, and public health officials *(pictured here measuring the head of a villager in the 1930s).*

Other medical officials in the United States had a more drastic solution. Mentally ill people should be sterilized (undergo surgery) to prevent them from ever having children. Between 1900 and 1935, at least thirty-five U.S. states passed laws authorizing the sterilization of people in mental asylums. California was one of the leaders in the effort, sterilizing twenty thousand individuals from 1909 to the early 1960s. In total, about sixty-five thousand Americans—including African American women, Native Americans, and criminals—were subjected to this extreme measure. Most states finally outlawed compulsory (forced) sterilization in the mid-1900s.

Darwin's legacy?

Social Darwinism affected the lives of millions of people. The eugenics movement in particular caused great suffering. Were these extreme ideas and movements a direct outcome of Charles Darwin's scientific theories?

Natural selection provided a framework for Social Darwinism, but many other current ideas contributed to the movement. "Survival of the fittest" became a slogan that represented these varied themes. Darwin had developed his theory of natural selection with great care, using scientific evidence to support and explain it. The ideas of Social Darwinism extended the theory into areas far beyond the world of science.

EUGENICS AT WAR

During the first decades of the 1900s, Germany set up programs to prevent mentally impaired people from reproducing. In 1933, the year that Adolf Hitler assumed power, the government passed the law for the Prevention of Genetically Diseased Offspring. Under this law, more than three hundred thousand people with severe mental or physical disabilities were sterilized. In 1939 the sterilization program became part of a larger Nazi plan to eliminate the "unfit" from German society. This plan eventually led to the horrors of the Holocaust during World War II (1939–1945), in which millions of Jews and other minority groups were killed in concentration camps.

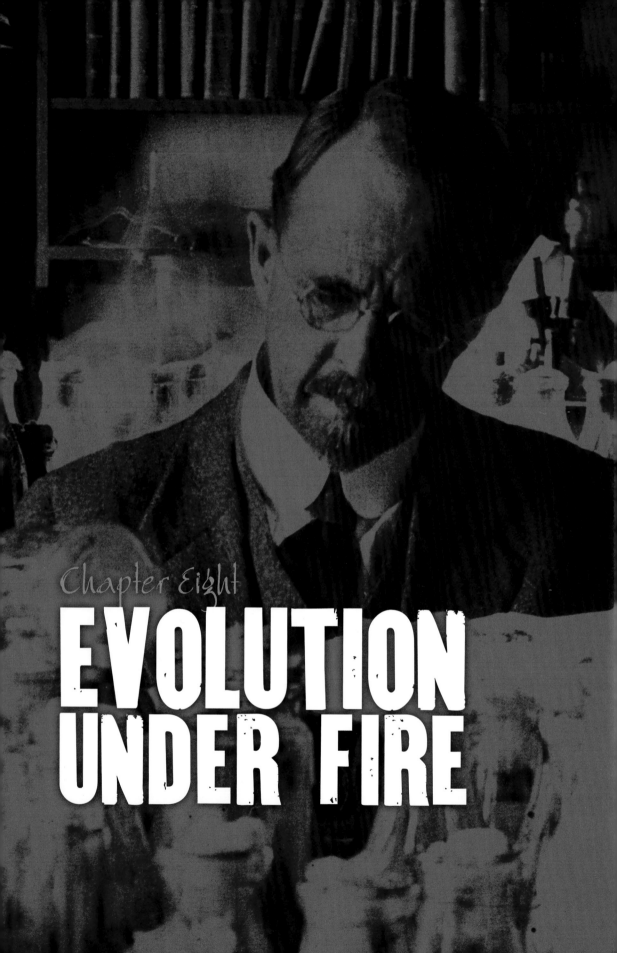

Chapter Eight

EVOLUTION UNDER FIRE

In the 1900s, Darwin's theory of evolution was given new life and restored to its important position in the world of science. During this same period, evolution came under a fierce new attack.

In the early decades of the century, continued research in the field of genetics produced solid evidence for the laws of genetic inheritance first discovered by Gregor Mendel. By the 1940s, a new generation of scientists realized that modern genetic theory could shed new light on Darwin's ideas about evolution. Research had shown that genes frequently change or mutate during the complex process of reproduction. These mutations create the variations that make up the raw material of natural selection. Based on this realization, many scientists found that they could agree on the basic ideas about evolution. In 1942 writer and biologist Julian Huxley, the grandson of Darwin's friend Thomas Huxley, published a book that described this agreement. He called it *Evolution: The Modern Synthesis.*

The ideas brought together in the modern synthesis were similar to those in *The Origin of Species.* New species evolve from older species through a process of gradual change. Natural selection is the primary mechanism that causes change. The modern version of Darwin's theory, sometimes called the neo-Darwinian synthesis, included many more details about how natural selection worked. Genetics had explained its basic operation but had also revealed how complicated a process it was.

"The evolutionary synthesis settled numerous old arguments once and for all, and thus opened the way for a discussion of entirely new problems. It was clearly the most decisive event in the history of evolutionary biology since the publication of *The Origin of Species* in 1859."

—**Ernst Mayr in** *The Growth of Biological Thought,* **1982**

Biologist and geneticist Thomas Hunt Morgan (facing page) **taught at Columbia University in New York in the early 1900s. He won a Nobel Prize in 1933 for his research on the role chromosomes play in heredity. He is pictured here in his famous fruit fly lab at Columbia.**

By the end of the 1900s and the beginning of the twenty-first century, almost all leading scientists had accepted the modified version of Darwin's theory of evolution. It became the basis of modern biology and influenced research in a wide range of fields. Charles Darwin had gotten it right after all.

THE CREATIONIST MOVEMENT

Despite the acceptance of evolution by most scientists, many people still viewed Darwin's theory with suspicion and disapproval. This was particularly true in the United States, where religious opposition to evolution was much more common during the 1900s than in Great Britain and Europe. In the second half of the century, American religious leaders and other public figures renewed the attack on evolution that had begun in 1859. Many of the arguments were the same, but opponents used some new weapons.

One of the primary arguments against evolution was based on a belief in the literal truth of the Bible. This had not been a major issue in the 1850s and the 1860s. During this period, many established Protestant churches did not insist that the account of creation in Genesis had to be accepted word for word.

During the 1900s, however, some churches began to shift to more conservative views. In the United States, new evangelical churches were established whose beliefs were based on a literal reading of the Bible. Leaders and members of these churches objected to the theory of evolution. They believed that it denied the word of God and the account of creation in Genesis. Those who opposed evolution for this reason called themselves creationists.

BATTLE FOR THE SCHOOLS

Religious opposition to evolution gathered force in the United States during the late 1900s. Church leaders, politicians, and public interest groups joined together in a common cause.

After the famous Scopes trial of 1925, Tennessee football coach and substitute teacher John Scopes *(right)* told a reporter that he had actually skipped teaching the lesson on evolution for which he had been brought to trial. For that reason, he claimed he was innocent of breaking a state law forbidding the teaching of evolution.

In the 1925 Scopes trial, Clarence Darrow *(center, with raised arm)* defended John Scopes's right to teach evolution. At the time, Darrow was the most famous trial lawyer in the United States. He had built a career defending striking workers, labor leaders, and anarchists.

"If science is based upon experience, then science tells us the message encoded in DNA must have originated from an intelligent cause. What kind of intelligent agent was it? On its own, science cannot answer this question; it must leave it to religion and philosophy."

—**Percival Davis and Dean Kenyon,** *Of Pandas and People,* **1993**

complicated to have evolved by the process of natural selection. In their view, the "irreducible complexity" of nature proves the existence of an all-powerful designer.

The major organization promoting intelligent design in the late 1990s was the Center for Science and Culture, established by law professor Phillip Johnson in 1996. A few scientists, including biochemist Michael Behe and mathematician William Dembski, joined forces with Johnson. Their goal was to convince the public that intelligent design is a valid scientific theory. To most scientists, however, ID is simply a more sophisticated version of creationism. In their view, "intelligent designer" is another name for the God of Christianity.

Like creationists before them, intelligent design proponents argued that public schools should present information about ID as well as Darwinian evolution in biology classes. They wanted schools to "teach the controversy" between the two theories. During the early 2000s, public school districts in several states began to allow ID into the science classroom.

In 2004 the school board in the town of Dover, Pennsylvania, passed a new provision. It required high school biology teachers to tell students that evolution was "just a theory." Teachers were also required to present intelligent design as another explanation for the origin of life. Some parents considered this action unconstitutional. They contacted the America Civil Liberties Union (ACLU), which sued the school district on their behalf.

During the trial in the U.S. District Court at the end of 2005,

This cartoon from the *Minneapolis StarTribune* pokes fun at the controversy surrounding teaching intelligent design in U.S. classrooms.

Law professor Phillip E. Johnson *(left)* and biochemistry professor Michael Behe *(right)* are modern proponents of the theory of intelligent design (ID). Johnson coined the term in the 1990s, and Behe was involved in a landmark 2005 court case in which he testified in support of ID.

A representative of the ACLU speaks at a news conference in 2004 at the state capitol in Harrisburg, Pennsylvania, during a lawsuit that challenged a state law requiring students to learn about ID and other alternatives to the theory of evolution.

Michael Behe and other proponents of ID appeared as witnesses for the defense. In his testimony, Behe said that "in the view of proponents of intelligent design theory, ID more accurately describes what we observe in nature than do competing theories."

ACLU lawyers had their own expert witnesses. Among them was Kenneth Miller, a cell biologist and textbook author who is a devout Catholic. Miller claimed that ID theory is based on "the argument from ignorance, which is to say that, because we don't understand something, we assume we never will, and therefore we can invoke a cause outside of nature, a supernatural creator or supernatural designer."

After hearing all the testimony, Judge John E. Jones handed down his decision. He declared that the Dover School Board's attempt to bring ID into the classroom was unconstitutional

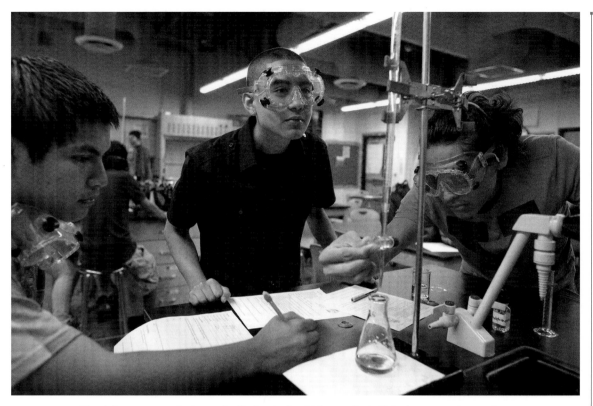

The debate over evolution and whether it should be taught in U.S. classrooms is ongoing, even though most scientists accept the accuracy of the theory.

because it violated the First Amendment of the Constitution. Jones said that "the overwhelming evidence at trial established that ID is a religious view, a mere re-labeling of creationism, and not a scientific theory."

In the Dover case, the opponents of evolution were defeated. They had lost this battle, but the war was not over.

CONCL

In the first decades of the twenty-first century, attitudes about the theory of evolution in the United States remain deeply divided. Despite the almost universal support of Darwinian evolution by scientists, a large percentage of the American public does not accept the theory. In a Gallup poll taken in 2012, 46 percent of those polled supported the statement that "God created human beings pretty much in their present form at one time within the last 10,000 years or so."

Support for evolution in other Western industrialized nations is generally higher than in the United States. Recent polls taken in Europe show this. A large majority of citizens in nations such as Sweden, France, and Britain think that humans developed from earlier species of animals.

Many U.S. scientists believe that the negative public attitude toward evolution results from a misunderstanding about the nature and role of science. In their view, science deals with the material world. It looks for natural causes that can be tested and studied. Religious or philosophical ideas provide a different way of looking at the world. These ideas can't be tested by science.

Many scientists have been able to accept evolutionary theory while still retaining their own personal religious beliefs. Theodosius Dobzhansky, one of the leaders in the neo-Darwinian synthesis, was a Russian Orthodox Christian. Dobzhansky called himself a creationist and an evolutionist. "Creation is not an event that happened in 4004 B.C.," he said. "It is a process that began some 10 billion years ago and is still under way."

Kenneth Miller, the cell biologist who testified at the Dover School trial in 2005, also finds no conflict between evolution and religion. In his testimony, he said, "I deeply care about my own religious beliefs and faith, and I also deeply care about science."

Miller insisted that while evolutionary theory is "fully compatible" with religion, "religious beliefs are not scientific, . . . they are philosophical, theological, and deeply personal."

There are some scientists who think that evolution and religion are incompatible. Richard Dawkins, a British biologist and well-known writer, is a representative of this group. His best-selling book *The God Delusion* (2006) presented his views about the conflict between evolutionary science and a belief in God. Other scientists such as Daniel Dennett and E. O. Wilson hold similar views.

Despite conflicting opinions about evolution and faith, all scientists agree that Darwin's theory is one of the foundations of modern science. It is an idea that cannot be ignored. The general public rejection of evolution in the United States has created a deep gulf between the world of science and the beliefs of many ordinary people. The controversy that began in 1859 with the publication of *The Origin of Species* continues.

"THE FUNDAMENTAL CORE OF CONTEMPORARY DARWINISM . . . IS NOW BEYOND DISPUTE AMONG SCIENTISTS. . . . NEW DISCOVERIES MAY CONCEIVABLY LEAD TO DRAMATIC . . . SHIFTS IN THE DARWINIAN THEORY, BUT THE HOPE THAT IT WILL BE 'REFUTED' BY SOME SHATTERING BREAKTHROUGH IS ABOUT AS REASONABLE AS THE HOPE THAT WE WILL RETURN TO A GEOCENTRIC VISION [THE BELIEF THAT THE EARTH IS THE CENTER OF THE UNIVERSE]."

—Daniel C. Dennett, *Darwin's Dangerous Idea*, 1995

ACTIVITY
CONSTRUCTING A POINT OF VIEW

With a small group (or on your own), read the concluding paragraph from the first edition of Darwin's *On the Origin of Species* *(below)*. Consider the addition of the words "by the Creator" in the second edition of the same text *(below)*. Does it change the meaning? If so, how? If not, why not?

Discuss your findings and write a paragraph or two that summarizes the group's opinion. If the group has differences of opinion, summarize those differences.

ON THE ORIGIN OF SPECIES (1ST ED., 1859)

It is interesting to contemplate a tangled bank, clothed with many plants of many kinds, with birds singing on the bushes, with various insects flitting about, . . . and to reflect that these elaborately constructed forms, so different from each other, . . . have all been produced by laws acting around us. . . . There is a grandeur to this view of life, with its several powers, having been originally breathed into a few forms or into one; and that whilst this planet has gone cycling on according to the fixed law of gravity, from so simple a beginning endless forms most beautiful and most wonderful have been, and are being evolved.

ON THE ORIGIN OF SPECIES (2ND ED., 1860)

It is interesting to contemplate a tangled bank, clothed with many plants of many kinds, with birds singing on the bushes, with various insects flitting about, . . . and to reflect that these elaborately constructed forms, so different from each other, . . . have all been produced by laws acting around us. . . . There is a grandeur to this view of life, with its several powers, having been originally breathed by the Creator into a few forms or into one; and that whilst this planet has gone cycling on according to the fixed law of gravity, from so simple a beginning endless forms most beautiful and most wonderful have been, and are being evolved.

GLOSSARY

BLENDED INHERITANCE: a theory of inheritance based on the idea that traits passed down by parents are mixed or blended together in their offspring

CATASTROPHISM: the theory that geological changes during Earth's history happened abruptly and were caused by catastrophic events such as floods

CREATIONISM: the belief that the universe and all living beings were created individually by a divine power. Most Christian creationists accept the account of creation presented in the Book of Genesis in the Bible.

DESCENT WITH MODIFICATION: a phrase used by Charles Darwin to describe gradual changes in organisms that produced new species. The word *evolution* gradually came to replace this term.

EUGENICS: a movement dedicated to the idea that human society could be improved by encouraging "fit" people to reproduce and discouraging or preventing the "unfit" from having children

FOSSILS: remains of ancient animals and plants that have been preserved in rock or soil

GEMMULES: units of inheritance that Darwin believed were produced by individual body cells. According to the theory of pangenesis, gemmules are sent to the reproduction organs and passed on to descendants.

GENES: the basic units of heredity. Genes are sections of deoxyribonucleic acid (DNA) that are carried on the chromosomes within the nucleus of a cell.

GERM PLASM: In August Weismann's theory of heredity, a material contained in chromosomes. Germ plasm allows genetic traits to be passed from parents to offspring.

INTELLIGENT DESIGN (ID): a belief based on the idea that the complex features of the natural world must have been created by an intelligent designer

LAMARCKISM: a theory of organic evolution originally developed by Jean-Baptiste Lamarck (1744–1829) in the early 1800s. An important feature of this theory was the idea that traits acquired during the lifetime of an organism could be passed on to descendants.

NATURAL SELECTION: the process by which organisms with traits favorable to their environment survive and reproduce. Those with unfavorable traits gradually die out.

NATURAL THEOLOGY: a belief that the evidence of design and function in the universe prove the existence of God. William Paley (1743–1805) advocated this view in the early 1800s.

NEO-DARWINIAN SYNTHESIS: the theory of evolution that combines Darwin's basic ideas about natural selection with modern genetics. Almost all biologists and many other scientists in the twenty-first century accept this theory.

PALEONTOLOGY: the science that studies the evidence of ancient life. It includes the study of fossils, comparative anatomy, geology, and other sciences.

PANGENESIS: Darwin's theory of inheritance, based on the belief that each body part produces specific genetic information that is sent to the reproductive organs

SEXUAL REPRODUCTION: a form of reproduction in which male sperm cells and female egg cells combine to create a new and unique organism. In forms of asexual (nonsexual) reproduction such as cloning, the new organism is an exact copy of the original.

SOCIAL DARWINISM: a general term used to apply biology to social and economic policies. Social Darwinism is based on the idea that competition between individuals and groups ensures that superior people will prevail over inferior people. The competition is viewed as necessary for human progress.

SPECIES: a group of closely related organisms capable of breeding together. Species is the basic category in the system of scientific classification developed by the Swedish naturalist Carl Linnaeus (1707–1778).

THEORY: a detailed explanation of some aspect of the natural world, based on a body of facts that have been confirmed through extensive observation and experiment

TRANSMUTATION: the theory of gradual organic change first developed by Jean-Baptiste Lamarck and Erasmus Darwin (1731–1802) in the early 1800s. The term *evolution*, which describes the same principle, was not commonly used until the late 1800s.

UNIFORMITARIANISM: the theory that changes in Earth's history took place gradually and were caused by the same slow-acting natural forces that can be observed in the present

SOURCE NOTES

4. Gen. 1: 1, 20, 21, 25 (King James Version).

5. Charles Darwin, *The Annotated Origin: A Facsimile of the First Edition of On the Origin of Species* (Cambridge, MA: Belknap Press of Harvard University, 2009), 6.

6. Ibid., 490.

13. Charles Darwin, *The Autobiography of Charles Darwin: 1809–1882*, ed. Nora Barlow (New York: W. W. Norton & Company, 2005), 21.

13. Ibid., 36.

14. Ibid., 49.

15. Ibid., 428.

16. Ibid., 60.

17. Ibid., 64.

18. Charles Darwin, *The Voyage of the Beagle* (New York: Modern Library, 2001), 270.

20. Ibid., 337.

24. Ibid.

25. Charles Darwin, Transmutation Notebook B, 73, available online at *The Complete Works of Darwin Online*, ed. John van Wyhe, n.d., http: // darwin-online.org.uk/contents /frameset?itemID=CULDAR121.- &viewtype=text&pageseq=1 (August 29, 2012).

27. Thomas Malthus, *An Essay on the Principle of Population* (London: J. Johnson, 1798), 114, *Library of Economics and Liberty*. http.//www .econlib.org/library/Malthus/malPop .html (July 18, 2012).

28. Charles Darwin, *Autobiography*, 195.

29. Emma Darwin, letter to Charles Darwin, no. 441, November 21–22, 1838, Darwin Correspondence Project, 2012, http://www .darwinproject.ac.uk/entry-441 (August 1, 2012).

29. Charles Darwin, *Autobiography*, 199.

30. George Darwin, quoted in David Quammen, *The Reluctant Mr. Darwin* (New York: W. W. Norton Company, 2006), 93.

31. Charles Darwin, letter to Leonard Jenyns, no. 782, October 12, 1844, Darwin Correspondence Project, 2012, http://www.darwinproject .ac.uk/entry-782 (August 14, 2012).

31. Charles Darwin, letter to Joseph Hooker, no. 729, January 11, 1844, Darwin Correspondence Project, 2012, http://www.darwinproject .ac.uk/entry-729 (August 21, 2012).

35. Charles Darwin, letter to Charles Lyell, no. 2,285, June 18, 1858, Darwin Correspondence Project, 2012, http://www.darwinproject .ac.uk/entry-2285 (August 21, 2012).

36. Charles Darwin, letter to Charles Lyell, no. 2,294, June 25, 1858, Darwin Correspondence Project, 2012, http://www.darwinproject. ac.uk/entry-2294 (August 18, 2012).

36. Charles Darwin, letter to Joseph Hooker, no. 2,450, April 7, 1859, Darwin Correspondence Project, 2012, http://www.darwinproject .ac.uk/entry-2450 (August 24, 2012).

36. Charles Darwin, letter to William Fox, no. 2,493, September. 23, 1859, Darwin Correspondence Project, 2012, http://www.darwinproject .ac.uk/entry-2493 (August 18, 2012).

37. Charles Darwin, *Annotated Origin*, 459.

37. Ibid., 80-81.

37. Ibid., 171.

39. Ibid., 489, 490.

41. J. R. Leifchild, review of *The Origin of Species* in the *Athanaeum*, no. 1,673 (November 19, 1859), available online in *The Complete Works of Darwin* Online, ed. John van Wyhe, n.d., http: //darwin-online.org.uk /contents/frameset?viewtype=text& itemID=A506&pageseq=1 (August 30, 2012).

41. Charles Lyell, letter to Charles Darwin, no. 2,501, October 3, 1859, Darwin Correspondence Project, 2012, http://www.darwinproject .ac.uk/entry-2501 (August 13, 2012).

41. Joseph Hooker, letter to Charles Darwin, no. 2,579, December 12, 1859, Darwin Correspondence Project, 2012, http://www .darwinproject.ac.uk/entry-2579 (August 7, 2012).

42. Alfred Russel Wallace, to a friend, quoted in Janet Browne, *Charles Darwin: The Power of Place* (Princeton, NJ: Princeton University Press, 2002), 140.

42. Adam Sedgwick, letter to Charles Darwin, no. 2,545, November 24, 1859, Darwin Correspondence Project, 2012, http://www .darwinproject.ac.uk/entry-2545 (August 25, 2012).

45. Thomas Huxley, to Samuel Wilberforce, from reports at a meeting in Oxford, quoted in Janet Browne, *Charles Darwin: The Power of Place* (Princeton, NJ: Princeton University Press, 2002), 122.

45. Joseph Hooker, letter to Charles Darwin, no. 2,852, July 2, 1860, Darwin Correspondence Project, 2012, http://www.darwinproject .ac.uk/entry-2852 (August 13, 2012).

48. Charles Darwin, letter to Asa Gray, no. 2,998, November 26, 1860, Darwin Correspondence Project, 2012, http://www.darwinproject. ac.uk /entry-2998 (August 17, 2012).

48. Charles Darwin, *Autobiography*, 73.

49. William Paley, *Natural Theology or, Evidences of the Existence and Attributes of the Deity.* 12th ed. (London: J. Faulder, 1809), 537, available online at *The Complete Works of Darwin Online*, ed. John van Wyhe, n.d., http: //darwin-online.org .uk/contents/frameset&itemID=A142 &viewtype=text&pageseq=1 (August 31, 2012).

49. Charles Darwin, *Autobiography*, 488.

51. Robert FitzRoy, letter to a friend, quoted in Janet Browne, *Charles Darwin: The Power of Place* (Princeton, NJ: Princeton University Press, 2002), 94.

52. Charles Darwin, *Annotated Origin*, 167.

55. J. Fiske, (Obituary of) Charles Darwin, *Atlantic Monthly* 49, no. 296 (June 1882), available online at *The Complete Works of Darwin Online*, ed. John van Wyhe, n.d., http://darwin-online.org.uk/contents/frameset&itemID=A82&viewtype=text&pageseq=1 (August 30, 2012).

56. Charles Darwin, *Annotated Origin*, 205.

62. Charles Darwin, *Autobiography*, 90.

64. William Graham Sumner, *The Challenge of Facts and Other Essays* (New Haven, CT: Yale University Press, 1914), 90.

67. Ernst Mayr, *The Growth of Biological Thought: Diversity, Evolution, and Inheritance* (Cambridge, MA: Belknap Press of Harvard University, 1982), 569.

72. Percival Davis and Dean Kenyon, *Of Pandas and People: The Central Question of Biological Origins* (Dallas: Haughton Publishing Company, 1989), 7.

74. Michael Behe, expert witness statement, in *Kitzmiller v. Dover Area School District*, available online at National Center for Science Education, 2012, http://www.ncse.com/files/pub/kitzmiller/expert_reports/2005-03-24_Behe_expert_report_D.pdf (September 2, 2012)

74. Kenneth Miller, testimony, in *Kitzmiller v. Dover Area School District*, available online at National Center for Science Education, 2012, http://www.ncse.com/files/legal/kitzmiller/trial_transcripts/2005_0926_day1_pm.pdf (September 2, 2012)

75. Judge John E. Jones, decision, in *Kitzmiller v. Dover Area School District*, available online at National Center for Science Education, 2012, http://ncse.com/files/pub/kitzmiller/highlights/2005-12-20_Kitzmiller_decision.pdf (September 2, 2012), 139.

76. Frank Newport, *In U.S., 46% Hold Creationist View of Human Origins*, Gallup Politics, June 1, 2012, http://www.gallup.com/poll/155003/hold-creationist-view-human-origins.aspx, (August 30, 2012).

76. Theodosius Dobzhansky, "Nothing in Biology Makes Sense Except in the Light of Evolution," *American Biology Teacher* 35 (1973): 26.

77. Miller, testimony, in *Kitzmiller v. Dover Area School District*.

77. Daniel C. Dennett, *Darwin's Dangerous Idea: Evolution and the Meaning of Life* (New York: Simon and Schuster Paperbacks), 20.

78. Charles Darwin, *Annotated Origin*, 489–490.

78. Ibid.

SELECTED BIBLIOGRAPHY

Bowler, Peter J. *Evolution: The History of an Idea*. Berkley: University of California Press, 2003.

Brockman, John, ed. *Intelligent Thought: Science versus the Intelligent Design Movement*. New York: Vintage Books, 2006.

Browne, Janet. *Charles Darwin: The Power of Place*. Princeton, NJ: Princeton University Press, 2002.

———. *Charles Darwin: Voyaging*. New York: Alfred K. Knopf, 1995.

———. *Darwin's Origin of Species: A Biography*. New York: Atlantic Monthly Press, 2006.

Darwin, Charles. *The Annotated Origin: A Facsimile of the First Edition of On the Origin of Species*. Cambridge, MA: Belknap Press of Harvard University, 2009.

———. *The Autobiography of Charles Darwin: 1809–1882*. Edited by Nora Barlow. New York: W. W. Norton & Company, 2005.

———. *The Descent of Man, and Selection in Relation to Sex*. London: John Murray, Abermarle Street, 1871. Available online at *The Complete Works of Darwin* Online. Edited by John van Wyhe. N.d. http: //darwin-online.org.uk/contents/frameset?itemID=F937.1&viewtype=text&pageseq=1 (September 3, 2012).

———. *The Variations of Animals and Plants under Domestication*. London: John Murray, 1868. Available online at *The Complete Works of Darwin*

Online. Edited by John van Wyhe, N.d. http: //darwin-online.org.uk/contents/frameset?itemID=F877.1&viewtype=text&pageseq=1 (September, 3,2012).

———. *The Voyage of the Beagle*. New York: Modern Library, 2001.

Darwin, Erasmus. *Zoonomia; or, the Laws of Organic Life*. Boston: Thomas and Andrews, 1803. Available online at Project Gutenberg. N.d. http://www.gutenberg.org/files/15707/15707-h/15707-h.htm (August 29, 2012).

Darwin Correspondence Project. 2012. http://www.darwinproject.ac.uk (August 10, 2012).

Davis, Percival, and Dean Kenyon. *Of Pandas and People: The Central Question of Biological Origins*. Dallas: Haughton Publishing Company, 1989.

Dawkins, Richard. *The Greatest Show on Earth: The Evidence for Evolution*. New York: Free Press, 2009.

Dennett, Daniel C. *Darwin's Dangerous Idea: Evolution and the Meanings of Life*. New York: Simon & Schuster Paperbacks, 1995.

Desmond, Adrian, and James Moore. *Darwin: The Life of a Tormented Evolutionist*. New York: W. W. Norton & Company, 1991.

Dobzhansky, Theodosius. "Nothing in Biology Makes Sense Except in the Light of Evolution." *American Biology Teacher*, March 1973, 25–29.

Gould, Stephen Jay. *Ever Since Darwin: Reflections in Natural History.* New York: W. W. Norton & Company, 1977.

Hofstadter, Richard. *Social Darwinism in American Thought.* New York: George Braziller, 1955.

Kevles, Daniel J. *In the Name of Eugenics: Genetics and the Uses of Human Heredity.* New York: Alfred A. Knopf, 1985.

Malthus, Thomas. *An Essay on the Principle of Population.* London: J. Johnson, 1798, 114. Available online at *Library of Economics and Liberty.* http://www.econlib.org/library /Malthus/malPop.html (August 6, 2012).

Mayr, Ernst. *The Growth of Biological Thought: Diversity, Evolution, and Inheritance.* Cambridge, MA: Belknap Press of Harvard University, 1982.

———.*What Evolution Is.* New York: Basic Books, 2001.

National Academy of Sciences. *Science, Evolution, and Creationism.* Washington, DC: National Academies Press, 2008.

Paley, William. *Natural Theology or, Evidences of the Existence and Attributes of the Deity.* 12th ed. (London: J. Faulder, 1809), 537, available online at *The Complete Works of Darwin Online,* ed. John van Wyhe, n.d., http://darwin-online.org.uk /contents/frameset?itemID=A142& viewtype=text&pageseq=1 (August 31,2012).

Pearson, Karl. *The Grammar of Science.* London: A and C Black, 1911.

Petto, Andrew J., and Laurie R. Godfrey, eds. *Scientists Confront Creationism: Intelligent Design and Beyond.* New York: W. W. Norton & Company, 2007.

Quammen, David. *The Reluctant Mr. Darwin.* New York: W. W. Norton Company, 2006.

Sumner, William Graham. *The Challenge of Facts and Other Essays.* New Haven, CT: Yale University Press, 1914.

SUGGESTED READING

Ashby, Ruth. *Young Charles Darwin and the Voyage of the Beagle*. Atlanta: Peachtree, 2009.

Ballen, Karen Gunnison. *Decoding Our DNA: Craig Venter vs the Human Genome Project*. Minneapolis: Twenty-First Century Books, 2013.

Barlow, Nora, ed. *The Autobiography of Charles Darwin: 1809–1882*. New York: W. W. Norton & Company, 2005.

Bruno, Leone. *Origin: The Story of Charles Darwin*. Greensboro, NC: Morgan Reynolds Pub., 2009.

Darwin, Charles. *On the Origin of Species: The Illustrated Edition*. Edited by David Quammen. New York: Sterling Publishing, 2008.

———. *The Voyage of the Beagle*. New York: Modern Library, 2001.

Fleisher, Paul. *Evolution*. Minneapolis: Twenty-First Century Books, 2006.

Gamlin, Linda. *Evolution*. New York: DK Publishing, 2009.

Heiligman, Deborah. *Charles and Emma: The Darwins' Leap of Faith*. New York: Henry Holt and Company, 2009.

Johnson, Rebecca L. *Genetics*. Minneapolis: Twenty-First Century Books, 2006.

King, David C. *Charles Darwin*. New York: DK Publishing, 2007.

Lasky, Kathryn. *One Beetle Too Many: The Extraordinary Adventures of Charles Darwin*. Somerville, MA: Candlewick Press, 2009.

Patent, Dorothy Hinshaw. *Charles Darwin: The Life of a Revolutionary Thinker*. New York: Holiday House, 2001.

Silverstein, Alvin, Virginia Silverstein, and Laura Silverstein Nunn. *Adaptation*. Minneapolis: Twenty-First Century Books, 2008.

———. *DNA*. Minneapolis: Twenty-First Century Books, 2009.

Yannuzzi, Della. *Gregor Mendel: Genetics Pioneer*. New York: Franklin Watts, 2004.

WEBSITES

About Darwin
http://www.aboutdarwin.com/
Created by a historian of science, this website presents the "life and times of Charles Darwin," including a timeline and many photographs.

Evolution
http://www.pbs.org.wgbh/evolution/
Based on a public television series, the site includes clips from the TV episodes and related articles. The section on Darwin's diaries and notebooks is particularly interesting.

Understanding Evolution
http://www.evolution.berkeley.edu/
This website was developed by the University of California Museum of Paleontology and the National Center for Science Education. It includes an "Evolution 101" course and an "interactive investigation" on the evolution of insects and other arthropods.

INDEX

PHOTO ACKNOWLEDGMENTS

The images in this book are used with the permission of: Library of Congress, pp. 1 (LC-DIG-ggbain-03485), 6 (LC-DIG-ggbain-03485), 22 (LC-USZ62-98523); © Natural History Museum, London/SPL/Photo Researchers, Inc., pp. 2-3 (backgound), 10 (background), 21 (bottom), 34 (top); © Universal History Archive/Universal Images Group/Getty Images, pp. 4-5, 35; © Universal Images Group/SuperStock, p. 7; Courtesy of the National Library of Medicine, pp. 10 (top), 12, 53, 59 (left), 60; © Todd Strand/Independent Picture Service, pp. 10 (bottom), 59 (right); © Science Source/Photo Researchers, Inc., pp. 13, 49 (bottom), 51 (top left); © Apic/Hulton Archive/Getty Images, p. 15 (top left); © Paul D. Stewart/SPL/Photo Researchers, Inc., pp. 15 (top right), 21 (top), 49 (top), 51 (top right); © Loop Images/SuperStock, p. 15 (bottom); © Pictorial Press Ltd./Alamy, p. 17 (top left); © SPL/Photo Researchers, Inc., p. 17 (top right); © Hulton Archive/Getty Images, pp. 17 (bottom), 44 (left); © The Natural History Museum, London, pp. 19 (top), 32, 34 (bottom), 38; © The Bridgeman Art Library, p. 19 (bottom); © English Heritage Picture Library, pp. 25, 28, 30, 33, 51 (bottom); © Time & Life Pictures/Mansell/Getty Images, p. 40; © Mario Tama/Getty Images, p. 44 (right); © iStockphoto.com/Giorgio Magini, p. 46; © Spencer Arnold/Hulton Archive/Getty Images, p. 54; © Carl De Souza/AFP/Getty Images, p. 56; American Philosophical Society, p. 64 (top); © ullstein bild/The Image Works, p. 64 (bottom); Courtesy of the Archives, California Institute of Technology, p. 66; © Gamma-Keystone via Getty Images, p. 69 (top); © Bettmann/CORBIS, p. 69 (bottom); © Topical Press Agency/Hulton Archive/Getty Images, p. 70; © Steve Sack, p. 73 (top); UC Berkeley School of Law, p. 73 (bottom left); AP Photo/Rick Smith, p. 73 (bottom right); AP Photo/Carolyn Kaster, p. 74; © Bob Daemmrich/The Image Works, p. 75.

Back cover: Library of Congress (LC-USZ61-104).

Main body text set in Janson Text LT Std 55 Roman 12/16.
Typeface provided by Monotype Typography.

ABOUT THE AUTHOR

Sylvia A. Johnson is an award-winning writer of nonfiction books for young adults. She has written on many different topics, ranging from the lives of crows to the Spanish conquest of Mexico. The history and culture of Mexico are among her special interests, and she has made frequent visits to the colonial cities and archaeological sites of that country. She makes her home in Minneapolis, Minnesota.